THE CHRISTIAN FAMILY AS A DOMESTIC CHURCH

VOLUME TWO: THE FAMILY AS A DOMESTIC CHURCH: EXPERIENCES FROM
THE WORLD MEETING OF FAMILIES

DEDICATION OF THIS WORK TO THOSE WHO HONOUR
THE HOLY FAMILY OF JESUS, MARY AND JOSEPH

This book is lovingly dedicated to all those who
honour Jesus, Mary and Joseph,
the Holy Family of Nazareth
by putting their virtues
into practice and
taking positive steps
towards the development
and promotion of family
spirituality in the world.

BLESSINGS: May the blessings of the Almighty God
rain abundantly on those who use this book profitably
and make sacrifices to present any or the three volumes
of the same book as special gifts to families of their choice
for the purpose of bringing them nearer to our merciful Father in heaven.

THE CHRISTIAN FAMILY AS A DOMESTIC CHURCH

Volume Two
The Family as a Domestic Church:
Experiences From the
World Meeting of Families

Sir David Osunde

ISBN 978 1 80097 023 6

10 9 8 7 6 5 4 3 2 1

Nihil Obstat: Rev. Dr Victor Onwukeme MSP, former Rector of the
National Missionary Seminary of St Paul, Gwagwalada, Abuja,
and former Superior General of the Missionary Society of St Paul
Imprimatur: † Most Rev. Dr Augustine Akubeze
Archbishop/Metropolitan of the See of Benin City,
President of the Catholic Bishops' Conference of Nigeria (CBCN)

Designed by Colette Dower
Cover photo: An African American, Tyree Davis, based in Miami is always in
love with his African roots. Here he happily displays the Nigerian flag at the
opening session of the World Meeting of Families in Milan, Italy, in 2012.
Printed in the Republic of Ireland by SPRINT-print Ltd, Dublin

*This book is printed on paper made from the wood pulp of managed
forests. For every tree felled, at least one tree is planted, thereby
renewing natural resources.*

ENQUIRIES: For all enquiries on how to reach the Holy Family Society for the
purposes of starting a new branch in your diocese, parish, Mass centre, etc., and for
registering new members/inaugurating new branches in your domain as well as placing
orders for your spiritual tools such as Prayer books, Novena Book, Song Book, Holy
Family Society Constitutions, sacramentals, etc., please contact the National Secretariat
of the society through her email address: hfsnationalsecretariat@yahoo.com

Contents

Foreword

The second volume of the book of Sir David Osunde and his wife, Dame Mary-Joan Osunde, on the Christian Family as a Domestic Church, is one of those books one opens to read and does not want to stop until one comes to the conclusion. In a very simple and straightforward language and manner, the authors, sharing their own experiences of a happy marriage and those of their children, though sometimes not without 'worries and anxieties', which they deposit 'at the foot of the altar' during the Holy Mass and daily prayer, describe the joy of a Christian family life, as they themselves have lived it during the last forty-five years of their married life.

During my mission as Apostolic Nuncio to Nigeria from 2010 to 2016, I came to know this couple of Papal Knights and participated at some of their different pastoral initiatives and social activities within the Holy Family Society and in favour of persons with disabilities. I was, therefore, very delighted when they announced to me the publication of this book on the theme of their long-experienced apostolate.

The lockdown during this period of the coronavirus pandemic, COVID-19, which has obliged churches to close down for several months, has confirmed even more the importance and necessity of cultivating the domestic church in this age of new evangelisation in a secularised world, where the traditional Christian family values are also being challenged.

This book contains a lot of resource materials put together in harmony to help any married couple begin to behave in such a way that their marriage becomes a 'mini-heaven' and not a 'mini-hell' or a burden that unfortunately ends up in divorce. I would highly and warmly recommend this book especially to young Christian couples who desire to live and give witness of a happy marriage, as well as to priests and to all those involved in the apostolate of preparing future marriages or directing retreats or seminars of married couples and their families.

Reading this book, one is reminded of 'the right words, spoken at the right time' that 'daily protect and nurture love' in a Christian family, the domestic church, as Pope Francis advises in his Post-Synodal Apostolic Exhortation *Amoris Laetitia,* no. 133 and in the Apostolic Exhortation *Gaudete et Exsultate,* nos. 142–145, on the universal Call to Holiness in Today's World: 'Sharing the word and celebrating the Eucharist together fosters fraternity and makes us a holy and missionary community'.[1]

The authors are convinced that 'The only way to holiness is to make personal sacrifices right from the comfort of one's home, giving quality time for prayers, just like the Apostles of Christ did'; which, in fact, is the victory of the culture of love over the culture of death in our world.

† Archbishop Augustine Kasujja
Apostolic Nuncio to the Kingdom of Belgium
& to the Grand Duchy of Luxembourg
Brussels, 8 September 2020

---

[1] Pope Francis, Post-Synodal Apostolic Exhortation *Amoris Laetitia*, 133, Vatican, 2016; Pope Francis, Apostolic Exhortation *Gaudete et Exsultate*, 142, Vatican, 2018.

Preface

One of the richest images and most apt descriptions of the Christian family is the image of the family as a domestic church. This term has been vigorously employed in the documents and writings of the Church. The family is a primary and central unit of society. If a society is healthy, it is because the family is healthy and if the society is sick, it is a reflection of the maladies in families, since a society is no less than a combination of families.

The family is described as a domestic church for several reasons. One of the documents of the Second Vatican Council, *Lumen Gentium*, describes the family as a domestic church because it is the first habitat in which the child learns about God. It states that: 'From the wedlock of Christians there comes the family, in which new citizens of human society are born, who by the grace of the Holy Spirit received in baptism are made children of God, thus perpetuating the people of God through the centuries'.[1]

In other words, everyone is born into a family and there, they are first taught and educated about God. The Church is a place of contact and connection with God and this contact and connection is first nurtured in the family, hence, the family is regarded as a

[1] Pope Paul VI, Dogmatic Constitution on the Church *Lumen Gentium*, 11, Vatican, 1964

domestic church. *Lumen Gentium* puts it clearly again: 'In it, parents should, by their word and example, be the first preachers of the faith to their children; they should encourage them in the vocation which is proper to each of them, fostering with special care vocation to a sacred state'.[2]

St Augustine's famous phrase: 'vero vides Trinitatem, si caritatem vides', or 'if you see charity, yes indeed, you see the Trinity', justifies further a sense in which the family is a domestic church.[3] The family is the first place of love and charity. Hence, there is God, and this community of love can be called a domestic church.

Pope emeritus, Benedict XVI explains another sense in which the family is regarded as a domestic church. The Pope in his address to the participants at the Plenary Assembly of the Pontifical Council for Families and the thirtieth anniversary of *Familiaris Consortio*, 1 December 2011, notes that: 'The family is indeed the *way* of the Church because it is the "human space" of our encounter with Christ. Spouses, "not only receive the love of Christ and become a saved community, but they are also called upon to communicate Christ's love to their brethren, thus becoming a saving community"'.[4] The family in this sense is understood as a saving community or in a deeper sense, a life-saving community.

Pope Francis further appeals to this image of the family as a domestic church. He says: 'Families are the domestic church, where Jesus grows; he grows in the love of spouses, he grows in the lives of children. That is why the enemy so often attacks the family. The devil does not want the family; he tries to destroy it, to make sure that there is no love there'.[5]

---

[2] Pope Paul VI, *Lumen Gentium*, 11
[3] St Augustine of Hippo, *De Trinitate*, VIII, 8, *c.* 1200–99
[4] Pope John Paul II, Apostolic Exhortation *Familiaris Consortio*, 49, Vatican, 1981
[5] Pope Francis, *Address to Participants in the 37th National Convocation of the Renewal in the Holy Spirit*, Rome, 2014

Furthermore, in his General Audience, 13 November 2019, Pope Francis deepens this understanding of the family as a domestic church, focusing on the married couple Aquila and Priscilla (or Prisca) in Acts of the Apostles, chapter eighteen, and how they opened their doors not only to the Apostles but also to the brothers and sisters in Christ. He says: 'Indeed, Paul can speak of a "community that gathers in their house" (cf. 1 Cor 16:19), which becomes a "house of the Church", a *domus ecclesiae*", a place in which to listen to the Word of God and celebrate the Eucharist'. The house of Aquila and Prisca becomes a place of catechesis (cf. Acts 18:26), thus, making it a domestic church.

The rich understanding of the family as a domestic church, through the various writings and documents of the Church both recognises the place of the family in the new evangelisation and its place in society. This recognition leaves several demands on the family. Therefore, for the family to live out its mission and vision, it needs to be constantly renewed. This renewal is even more exigent because families today are fiercely under attack from different sides. Just the way Satan wages war against the Church of Christ on earth, so too, he wages war against the family as a domestic church.

The attacks against the family seek to destroy the witness of Christian marriage as well as to destroy and disfigure God's plan for creation. These attacks on the family sometimes come in the form of different philosophies and ideologies that are promoted by contrary voices in the world. The challenges confronting the Christian family make the renewal for the Christian family a constant duty and a moral obligation.

This book by Sir David Osunde and Dame Mary-Joan Osunde, which is the second of a trilogy on *The Christian Family as a Domestic Church,* pursues the focus of the renewal of the Christian family in a special way. This second volume focuses on how the family can fully actualise its vision as a domestic church. Through lived experiences as a couple for over forty-five years and the experiences of other families, especially those from the World Meeting of Families in Philadelphia, the authors bring to the fore ideas on how to grow, develop, enliven and vivify the domestic church. This second volume, which almost seamlessly flows from the first, reflects deeply on particular directions and dimensions for growing a domestic church. In it, the authors seek to highlight the Christian character of the family and how the family can remain Christian and holy.

The book exposes some Christian principles that need to be imbibed by families if members of the family must remain true to their vocation of being witnesses of the Christian vocation.

The first volume of this book focuses on the foundational understanding of the family as a domestic church; how this can be fostered, how family members can be prepared in the journey of faith, and how to sustain the domestic church and her family members. It also focuses on the promotion of Christian values, how the family is a hub of evangelisation and how making good friends can help foster the vision of the family as a domestic church. These thoughts and expositions serve as a solid lever for this second volume. This volume, which is developed in ten chapters and written in a clear language with practical experiences to enhance understanding, dwells on how the domestic church can grow through the upholding of our shared Christian values and discipline.

The authors discuss the experiences and testimonies of couples and leaders of the faith who have instructed on how the domestic church should grow. Through a panorama of ideas, the authors focus particularly in Chapter One of this volume, how marriages can be renewed through prayers, and how the experience of staying with God brings prosperity in the family. It further exposes how marriages can be sustained through the Eucharist and also discusses what the Church expects of each family as a domestic church.

Chapters Two and Three expose in some detail the fundamentals of running a successful domestic church and what the Church expects of a functioning domestic church.

Through the informed contributions of bishops and priests, the authors reveal the theology of a domestic church, the focus on the missionary mandate of families and discuss how these impact on the overall mandate of evangelisation and making disciples of all nations (cf. Mt 28:19–20). Chapters Five and Six focus on the mission and theology of the domestic church, drawing on experiences from the Eighth World Meeting of Families in Philadephia, 2015 and the World Meeting of Families in Dublin, Ireland in 2018. These chapters focus on the themes for both world meetings: 'Love is Our Mission: The Family Fully Alive' and 'The Gospel of the Family: Joy for the World', respectively, drawing upon the rich discussions and proceedings from both world meetings to develop these chapters.

Chapters Six and Seven devote attention to the experiences of Christian families and individuals who have thrived on making their families a true example of a domestic church and to be spiritually beneficial for people in their household. These chapters discuss the role of the family in the new evangelisation. In Chapters Seven and Eight, God's injunction to the domestic church to be fruitful, multiply and fill the earth is discussed.

The ninth chapter provides recognition that a Christian family lives in a community of other people and families. Hence, there is a need to know how these people and communites impact on the growth of the domestic church. This makes the focus of this chapter both *ad rem*, and expedient.

The tenth chapter is retrospective, introspective and prospective of the discussions so far in *The Christian Family as a Domestic Church*. This chapter looks at the issues dealt with in Volume One, gives a summary of the discussions in the current volume and projects the expected topics of Volume Three. This makes it difficult to miss out in the flow of thought in this trilogy on the Christian family as a domestic church.

The concluding part of this volume offers rich traditional prayers for renewal and the building of a family spirituality.

The beauty of this particular volume on *The Christian Family as a Domestic Church* is the expanded vision it gives to the discussion on the Christian family, the practical domestication of the important theological and scriptural discussions on the subject matter, the sharing in the experiences of others, etc. The idea of storytelling has a great potential impact and source of strength for families that are becoming weary in their vocation as a Christian Family.

There are worthy examples for imitation led by other families that can help build the faith of others. It is in this sense of worthy emulation of virtuous acts of faith that the writer of the Letter to the Hebrews admonished: 'Remember your leaders who spoke the word of God to you. Consider the outcome of their way of life and imitate their faith' (Heb 13:7).

This book is simple and clear. It is theological, pastoral, scriptural and practical. It is written by a lay couple who have made sincere and consistent efforts in building their home as a domestic church and who have become evangelisers and missionaries to other families, both for their conversion and a reawakening of their role and vision as a domestic church.

This volume reaffirms the holiness and sanctity of family life as well as its role and place in the entire mission of Christ and the Church. This volume is truly a testament of the family as a domestic church. It is a manual of encouragement for all families and it is recommended for all families, especially those who seek a true renewal of their home and making it like that of the Holy Family of Jesus, Mary and Joseph.

Most Rev. Dr Augustine Akubeze
Archbishop/Metropolitan of the See of Benin City and
President, Catholic Bishops Conference of Nigeria (CBCN)

Review Comment

This book on the Christian family is a testament to the author's passionate commitment to the development of the family as the living domestic church. Written in plain language, it captures the pivotal role of the human family as the cradle of love as well as spirituality. It enunciates the godly attributes and virtues of the Christian home, the domestic, where every child should as a matter of necessity be groomed, grounded, and nurtured in matters of faith and morals.

Researchers in development psychology have long established that from birth to around age five the newborn child acquires most of the emotional, psychological and social characteristics that would follow him or her throughout their entire life. In essence, by age five, a significant amount of the child's temperaments, mannerisms, and idiosyncrasies, as well as the child's belief inclinations, would have been acquired through the child's close interaction with his or her parents, caregivers and neighbours.

At a later stage the growing person is subject to both negative and positive influences and pressures from the wider society, but the child's capacity to manage these external influences and pressures will depend largely on the extent to which a solid spiritual and moral foundation has earlier been laid at the family level. This is why the most opportune place for the child to develop the sense of God, the sense of love, the sense of right and wrong, as well as the attraction for good and revulsion for evil, etc., is the family, and not the regular Church or the school, which only begins to engage the child seriously around the age of five or six.

Yes, it is in the family that nuggets of faith, spirituality and morals are implanted on the growing infant. It is in the family that the elements of the life of Christian integrity, including decency, honesty, empathy, love of neighbour, perseverance, gratitude, and a deep sense of respect and reverence for the spiritual, the sacred and the divine are nurtured.

Sir David Osunde's new publication advocates that the age-old Church teaching on the family as the domestic church should be taken very seriously by all segments of the body of Christ, such that ever greater investment will be made towards equipping young families to take up the challenge of being domestic churches. The author's rich experience in the marriage and family apostolate, spanning many decades, has helped him to recognise and cherish all that is good and promising in the defence and protection of traditional Christian family values. His own experience in navigating life's opportunities and challenges has equipped him and his family with outstanding and exemplary lessons to pass on.

The author's lifelong passion for the all-round wellbeing of the Christian family has translated into producing this book, among his many other writings. His books and numerous articles on the family are inspired by the devoted involvement of himself and his wife of over forty-five years in multiple charities and philanthropy, in advancing the welfare and rights of the disabled, and in founding and coordinating the activities of the Holy Family Society in Nigeria, as well as his involvement in Christian family apostolate worldwide.

The book is enriched with soul-lifting testimonies of the participants and moderators at the global Christian family gatherings over the years. Indeed, the author's name has over time become synonymous with the family apostolate in Nigeria. In a world that is inexorably debased in an anti-life and anti-family culture, Sir Osunde and his family are to be highly commended for not only striving to pattern their family life after the example of the Holy Family of Jesus, Mary and Joseph, but also for taking on the Christian family as their life's mission.

This publication is highly recommended to all Christian families seeking to grow, to mature, and to succeed in their vocation to a life of Christian integrity here below, and everlasting union with God in heaven.

Rev. Fr George Ehusani,
Executive Director
Lux Terra Leadership Foundation
Abuja, Nigeria

Acknowledgements

This acknowledgement is unmistakably my special tribute to all those who worked towards the successful completion of the three volumes of this book. Let me make it clear from the start that the input from different sources for one volume inspired the preparation of the next volume, allowing the three volumes of the book to evolve naturally and miraculously. The miraculous completion of the three volumes on the domestic church within a space of nine months came to be because with God all things are possible.

It is important to note here that the writing of this book was never planned, hence it can be attributed to a miracle – a miracle in the sense that a thought suddenly came to the author that out of the coronavirus pandemic foisted on the world, something good can also come out of it.

With such a thought, I went into a quiet corner to ruminate about what to do next. It took another week or so before the directive and the direction came my way. The reader may want to know that I left Nigeria with my wife for the United States of America in November 2019, without planning to stay more than two months. Our main purpose for the visit was to await the arrival of our twenty-fifth grandchild as our daughter, Dr Marian Imaze Davis, was heavily pregnant. We were to wait there to conduct the baby's naming ceremony and participate in its baptismal ceremony in the Catholic Church before returning home in the New Year. This was our family plan. But God had a different plan for us. Our daughter, who was expecting her sixth child, had the baby on the 5 December 2019, and both the naming ceremony and the baby's baptism took place on the 29 December 2019. As it was a period of several celebrations, the days seemed to have moved quite fast, and before we could shout 'Alleluia' and 'Happy New Year' at many more occasions, we found ourselves already in the middle of January 2020.

Our daughter then advised us that before thinking of hurrying back to Nigeria, we should have a thorough medical examination, advising further that we should therefore move the dates on our air tickets forward. This was exactly what we did, only to discover that a few of our medical appointments were in February, March and April 2020. And before we could attend two of the different medical appointments, the coronavirus pandemic had set in. With the medical advice about social distancing, cancelling of travel plans, wearing of masks and restriction of movements to public places, we found that we had no choice than to settle in, watch the world from America, and pray for the coronavirus pandemic to disappear so that we could return to Nigeria.

This was not to come quickly and we were left with no other choice than to spend several hours on the phone every day to speak on a number of issues to different people in various parts of the world. It was at this point that the Holy Spirit entered, questioning through the inner voice: 'Why are you not making good use of the time I have given to you?'. This woke me from my deep slumber, and I personally settled in to undertake the task of writing a few chapters of my family experiences regarding the outcome of our effective use of our domestic church.

Looking around my room, I had only the Catechism of the Catholic Church, the Holy Family Society Prayer Books, the Community Holy Bible and other prayer books for different occasions. I immediately listed other books I might need for reference purposes for my daughter and her husband, Mr Tyree T. Davis, to place an order from the Pauline Bookshop in Miami. The books included: the Revised Standard Version Bible (Second Catholic Edition), Documents of Vatican II, and the Code of Canon Law.

It was only when these arrived, that I said to myself, that it could be possible that the coronavirus pandemic which was weekly claiming thousands of human lives might really bring about good things that would help to transform people's lives as well as bring sanctity to many. I also reasoned that my own work during the period could, with great personal sacrifices, help to bring Christian and non-Christian families nearer to God.

With such thoughts reverberating in my mind, I began to work on the first two chapters of the book based on the papers I had presented at conferences in the past. It became necessary for me to find who amongst our priests would be ready to travel the same route with me by spending quality time out of their busy schedules, to proofread and edit the scripts. After several contacts, I found a willing hand in the person of Rev. Fr Dr Victor Onwukeme, MSP, a former Rector of the Major Seminary of St Paul's Missionary Society, Gwagwalada, Abuja, and also a former Superior General of the congregation of the Missionary Society of St Paul (MSP).

His acceptance to travel the same route with me boosted my spiritual energy. I then decided to be more serious in moving from writing one chapter of the book to another. And I noticed that as I was finishing the first volume, I found that there were still many thoughts in my mind that were yet to be expressed. I felt it would be unwise to allow them to disappear.

So, I begged the Rev. Father to be kind enough to go through a second volume of the book with me, and he generously obliged without any hesitation, but made it clear to me that with several other works in his hand, I should not expect quick turn out of his proofreading.

With this settled, and knowing that the road was not clear for my wife and I to return to Nigeria, I then concentrated on the second volume which was then planned by me to incorporate the experiences of other families in the development, promotion and functioning of their domestic churches. I created room for other families to tell their individual stories. On the 6 and 7 of May 2020, I sent out two notices in addition to the previous one I had sent out on the 25 April 2020, requesting families to give their own testimonies on how the functioning of their domestic churches has helped them to develop their family spirituality. The message I sent out was titled:

> The Domestic Church: Why not make your family a part of the new mission on Global Family Evangelisation by giving your family testimony?

A part of the message I sent out read thus:

> A few days ago, (precisely on 25 April 2020), I intimated you through this WhatsApp platform about the intention of the Holy Family Society to put on the shelf for everyone, Christians and non-Christians alike, a new book on the domestic church as part of her efforts to impress on family members throughout the world to pay much more attention to the development of their family spirituality.
>
> This, we believe, Christians and non-Christians can do by, first and foremost, returning to their roots to make beneficial use of their homes as they organise themselves into family praying groups with a view to living the lives exemplified by the early Apostles and disciples of Christ. We also believe that some families among us already have a lot of experiences in organising their family devotions in the comfort of their homes, giving opportunities to everyone to develop themselves spiritually when they share the Word of God together, each day ...
>
> We therefore see it as a good thing for many growing families to learn from the initiatives of keen followers of Christ,

especially as regards the steps taken by them to keep their domestic churches functioning in the last ten or more years.

We will be so highly delighted to receive your genuine testimonies that we can take to the field to share joyously with others, with a view to winning more families for Christ.

Meanwhile, we are praying that enlightened Christian families reading the above will happily devote quality time to prepare their own testimonies which could form part of the legacies they will happily leave behind for future generations.

The above letter went through many group WhatsApp platforms to hundreds of families. After a number of reminders and after over three months of waiting for responses, only five families responded. Their stories are quite enriching and they are now good legacies that can spur many to positive action on improving their spiritual lives. This explains why their testimonies have been given prominent places in Volumes One and Two of this book. The families who contributed their very informative and inspiring family stories include:

(1) Dr David Ezeh, An Assistant Director, currently working in the Federal Ministry of Finance, Budget, and National Planning, Abuja. His family story can be found in Volume One, Chapter Four.

(2) Mrs Georgiana Ogochukwu Ogbutor, a retired Director in the Federal Civil Service of Nigeria. Her family story is in Volume Two, Chapter Seven.

(3) Mrs Ivonne Ruiz, An American housewife and a parishioner of St Brendan's Catholic Church, Miami, Florida. Her soul-captivating story is also in Volume Two, Chapter Seven.

(4) Clemetina Osayuwamen Osunde, Manager of a Secondary School Cafeteria in UK. Her own story is published in Volume Two, Chapter Six.

(5) Dr Mrs Marian Imaze Davis, a medical practitioner, with her own private medical practice in Miami, Florida. Similarly, her family story is incorporated in Volume Two, Chapter Seven.

There is no way I can thank them enough for their valuable contributions to the two volumes of this book. I must also use this opportunity to thank my fifteen-year-old granddaughter, Miss Glenda Oloke, who accompanied her mother, Mrs Augusta Ehinoma Oloke, to be in my entourage to attend the Ninth World Meeting of Families in Dublin, Ireland. She revealed in her powerful write-up, how her experiences in Dublin have strengthened her spiritual life. This can be found in Chapter Six of Volume Two of the book. It is advisable that parents should share her captivating testimony with their children.

Before using this same forum to thank all who made inestimable contributions to the production of these three volumes of work on the domestic church, let me quickly observe here that while I was still contemplating how to fully express my additional thoughts in Volume Two of the book, I realised that within four weeks of my requesting people to send in their own stories, Pope Francis was also sending out a similar message to people to mark the Fifty-fourth World Communications Day 2020, which was held throughout the world on Sunday 24 May 2020. He used the occasion to call all Mass Communicators and Christian families alike who have enviable stories about their lives to write them as such stories can become an 'appendix' to the bible.

Reading Pope Francis' message to mark the 2020 World Communications Day really spurred me on because a good part of it coincided with my thoughts about writing our faith-building stories to open doors for us in the new crusade to evangelise families. Be that as it may, it gave me a clear indication that God is really supportive of our new initiative, as he was using different people to send out similar messages. I personally got a further spiritual push to complete Volume Two and then moved on to put down my thoughts in Volume Three.

This is what brought about the three volumes of the work coming out at the same time. Is there any wonder that I attributed this to a miraculous undertaking and achievement? And does it also not reveal to the reader now that 'they who wait on the Lord shall renew their strength' (Is 40:31)?

Now it is time to give due honour to all who made the dream of producing the three volumes of this book on the domestic church a reality.

First and foremost, I wish to thank the almighty God for keeping all who participated in one way or the other in the production of the three volumes of this book safe and hearty during the period of the ravaging coronavirus pandemic. That I did not lose my bearing all through in my attempt to remember everything my wife and I did together to raise our children to be who they are today, I wish to give special thanks to her for being very supportive and productive.

Let me humbly state here that my wife, Dame Mary-Joan Osunde, whose activities at home, in the Church and in the community also attracted the Vatican, was considered for a Papal Honour of the Knight of St Sylvester by Pope Benedict XVI in 2005. This understandably shows that her care, loyalty and love for her husband, the Church and the community where she lives, are exemplary; I myself was similarly honoured as Papal Knight of St Sylvester by Pope John Paul II in 1992.

Considering what the Church Magisterium majorly did to direct our course in life as well as make the three volumes of the book available on the shelves, my family and I cannot really find the appropriate words to express adequately our heartfelt gratitude to Pope Francis and other Church leaders whose works I personally used copiously to buttress the various points I made in the three volumes of this book. Nor can I find the adequate words to express my immense thanks to our Church leaders who participated physically by contributing very valuable scripts that are incorporated in the three volumes of this book.

For the reader to know what came from our spiritual leaders who encouraged me to complete this work, I wish to simply refer to what each of them did specifically below, imploring them to kindly forgive me for not consulting them first before listing their names in this acknowledgment. Those among them who found time to quickly attend to our urgent requests as we solicited for their input include:

(1) Most Rev. Dr Augustine Akubeze, President of the Catholic Bishops' Conference of Nigeria, and the Archbishop of Benin City. He wrote the Preface for Volume Two of the book and also gave the Imprimatur for the same volume.

(2) Archbishop Augustine Kasujja, Apostolic Nuncio to the Kingdom of Belgium and to the Grand Duchy of Luxembourg. He wrote the Foreword for the same Volume Two.

(3) Most Rev. Dr Ignatius I. Kaigama, immediate past President of the Catholic Bishops' Conference of Nigeria, and the Catholic Archbishop of Abuja. He wrote the Preface for Volume Three and also gave the Imprimatur for the same Volume Three.

(4) Archbishop Fortunatus Nwanchukwu, Titular Archbishop of Aquaviva, Apostolic Nuncio to Trinidad and Tobago, in the Caribbean and Antilles. He wrote the Foreword for Volume Three.

(5) Most Rev. Dr Valerian M. Okeke, Archbishop of Onitsha. He wrote the Preface for Volume One and also gave the Imprimatur for the same Volume One.

(6) Most Rev. Dr Emmanuel Adetoyese Badejo, Bishop, Catholic Diocese of Oyo. He contributed a piece for Volume Two, Chapter Three, titled: 'Catholic Teaching About a Spirit-filled Domestic Church'.

(7) Most Rev. Dr Matthew Hassan Kukah, Bishop, Catholic Diocese of Sokoto. He contributed an incisive Comment on Volume Three which is at the beginning pages of the volume.

(8) Most Rev. Dr Jude Arogundade, Bishop, Catholic Diocese of Ondo. He wrote the Foreword for Volume One of the book.

(9) Most Rev. Dr Hilary Nanman Dachelem, Bishop, Catholic Diocese of Bauchi. He contributed a piece for Volume Three, Chapter Six, titled: 'Human Life: What Value to Attach – Does Mine Have a Meaning?'

(10) Rev. Fr Agbonkhianmeghe E. Orobator, SJ, President of the Jesuit Conference of Africa and Madagascar. He contributed a piece, titled: 'What the Church Expects of a Functioning Domestic Church'. This can be seen in Volume Two, Chapter Four of the book.

(11) Rev. Fr George Ehusani, Executive Director, Lux Terra Leadership Foundation. He wrote a Review Comment on Volume Two of the book.

(12) Rev. Fr Dr Victor Darlington, Parish Priest of Sacred Heart Catholic Church, Camberwell, SE5, 9QS, London, UK. He contributed a piece, titled: 'What the Church Expects of a Catholic Marriage'. His contribution forms part of the piece in Volume Two, Chapter One.

(13) Rev. Fr Cosmas Okechukwu Ebebe, PhD, FNPR. Lecturer, Department of Systemic Theology, Catholic Institute of West Africa, PortHarcourt, Nigeria. He did an insightful Appraisal of Volume Three of the book.

(14) Rev. Fr Oseni J. Osilama Ogunu, OMV, Dominican Institute, Ibadan and Founder/President of the Foundation for Human Rights and Development of African Christian Heritage. He wrote the Review Comment on Volume One.

(15) Rev. Fr Alexander Ekechukwu CSSp MA, University of London, England, Doctorate in Theology, Gregorian University, Rome, Italy. He wrote a comment on Volume One.

(16) Rev Fr. George Adimike, a PhD student in Rome who successfully completed his studies in Rome in 2020 and returned immediately to Nigeria to found what he described as the Faith-Inspiration Project. In spite of his mourning the death of his loving father, Chief Patrick Ndubueze Adimike, who went to his eternal reward on 11 June 2020, he still found time to help me to prepare a draft script that went out to one of our bishops.

(17) Rev. Fr John Paul Ojuikpai, Parish Priest, St Martin Catholic Church, Oso Edda, Abakaliki Diocese. He contributed a piece, requesting to be assisted in solving a marital problem in his parish in respect of a Christian who married two wives and now wants to reconcile himself with the Church for him to become once more, a communicant. His piece can be found in Volume Three, Chapter Two.

(18) Rev. Fr Osemhantie Okhueleigbe, Personal Secretary to Archbishop Patrick Ekpu, (Archbishop Emeritus of the Archdiocese of Benin City), contributed the first response to Rev. Fr John Paul Ojuikpai's request. This is also in Volume Three, Chapter Two of the book.

(19) Rev. Fr Henry Nkemakolam Emeka, Assistant Parish Priest, Christ the King Catholic Church, Magwi County, Eastern Equatorial State, South Sudan, sent in the second response regarding how to solve the problem of a polygamous husband who wants to reconcile himself with the Church and with God. His contribution is also in Volume Three, Chapter Two.

(20) As a way of giving a global look on the whole work I have completed, a Papal Knight of St Gregory the Great, Ambassador Martin Ihoeghian Uhumoibhi, OFR, KSJI, D.Phil. (Oxon), took quality time to appraise it, and he came up with a piece, titled: 'The Home as the First Congregation: An Appraisal of David Osunde's Theology of the Domestic Church'. This can be found in Volume One of the book.

There were others who read one or two volumes of the book and sent in their very inspiring comments. Their names cannot be individually mentioned here because of lack of space. Members of my family are joining me here to commend everyone to God for his special blessings. Our special commendation also goes to Rev. Fr Dr Victor Onwukeme, MSP, who made great sacrifices to proofread and edit the scripts contained in Volumes One, Two and Three of the book. I was like Oliver Twist, asking for more and more as I consumed his time with more and more work, sometimes making him read one script three times as we exchanged thoughts.

This exchange of thoughts helped a great deal in my redoing one of the chapters in Volume Three before both of us agreed that it met the standard of my previous works. For his insistence that the work be redone, I want to specially thank him for being a good teacher to me, otherwise the reader would have seen a good number of errors in this work.

In conclusion, I wish to thank all our children, grandchildren, brothers and sisters and other extended family relations who stayed in our home during their growing years for comporting themselves and adjusting to the rules in our home. It is true that some of you described it then as being in a sort of 'family military school'. But what many of you took out of the Christian home certainly impacted in you the virtues of discipline and agape love for your fellow human beings, in addition to the spiritual benefits we all shared in the home. These you should all now take along with you to affect the community where you live.

May the almighty God continue to bless the work of our hands as He directs each and every one of us, especially those who contributed immensely to the realisation of this project, to greater achievement.

Feast of St Joseph the Worker,
1 May 2020, Miami, Florida
Sir David E. Osunde
Founder/National Coordinator, Holy Family Society

1

Playing One's Part in a Domestic Church to Fulfil God's Purpose

Having, by the grace of God, enjoyed our own Catholic marriage over the last forty-five years, my wife and I can joyfully state with great conviction, that our Catholic sacramental marriage has been a great blessing to our entire family.

As our own special tribute to the marvellous work of God in our lives, we wish to state here that his special gift of seven children and twenty-five grandchildren to us within the forty-five years of our Catholic marriage has been our source of strength in carrying out the family apostolate work he has assigned to us.

As we look back, we can state, without any iota of doubt, that our ardent desire to follow God's plan for us, and our no-look-back stance in participating actively in a number of Church projects, and her spiritually uplifting programmes, have helped tremendously to keep our marriage young and as fresh as ever.

We can also state without any fear of contradiction, that the way we open up our home to all, be they Muslims, Christians, persons with disabilities, or the elderly, has contributed immensely to the freedom we enjoy in building up good relationships with people of different strata in life. This has also helped us tremendously in executing our various projects and programmes for persons with disabilities and the Holy Family Society.

These explain why people of goodwill, including bishops, priests, reverend sisters, persons with disabilities, and people of different faiths as well as our highly dependable staff always make great sacrifices to stand by us whenever we organise any event in or outside the country. From the bottom of our hearts, we say a big thank you to all, who have been so supportive of our marital life and the various spiritual projects we have executed so far.

Renewing Marriage With Prayers

It will not be out of place to state here that the prayers of thousands of people, especially the prayers of those living with disabilities have indisputably helped, in no small measure, to keep our marriage constantly renewed, with greater enthusiasm on our path to live a more prosperous life by attending to those in greatest need according to our means. So, as we live our daily life, we feel quite energised with great thoughts about living always for others, and making great efforts to attend morning Mass where we can have our worries and anxieties deposited at the foot of the altar.

We also feel strengthened by the fact that we are leaning solidly on Jesus, Mary and Joseph, the Holy Family of Nazareth. It must be mentioned here that we feel highly empowered on a daily basis as we effectively use the efficacious prayers in the Holy Family Society Prayer Book to have direct communion with God. It is only after prayer that we can joyfully step out of our home. These acts make us docile to the Holy Spirit, simple in our attitude and young in our appearance. Many cannot believe that both of us, husband and wife, are already seventy-three and sixty-eight years of age respectively. Is there any wonder why many people frequently ask us the secret of our simplicity and youthfulness?

Reflecting on God's injunction that we should 'be fruitful, multiply and fill the earth' (Gn 9:1), which will be appropriately addressed in Chapter Eight of this particular volume, let me quickly point out here that from the very beginning of our marriage, we had a good understanding of what it takes to be seen as a happily married couple. We also knew that in the area of procreation, we would need to cooperate fully with God in this special project for us to play our part well. So, before we had the first pregnancy in the family as we began our marital life, we had taken a decision that before and after sexual acts, we must raise our minds to God in prayer, imploring him to give us the child we deserve. Prayers before and after sexual intercourse as composed by us were constantly recited on the bed until we had the last baby, who, by the grace of God, is now a seasoned lawyer practicing in the UK. The remaining six children are professionals in their own right in the UK and America, hoping to return home after a few years of professional experience in other lands.

With the seven children and twenty-five grandchildren God has blessed us with as at the time of writing this, and with more grandchildren and great-grandchildren that will, by the grace of God, come in the future, we believe that God has greatly helped us in our family to play our own part, regarding his injunction: 'Be fruitful, multiply and fill the earth'. Everyone has what God has designed for him or her in this all-important enterprise of cooperating with him to fill the earth with human beings. Five of the distinct roles we can all play in this respect in order to carry out God's injunction are indicated in Chapter Eight of this book. So, the reader will discover what role he or she is playing in this respect.

Having played our own part in the act of procreation with a view to filling the earth, our immediate role now is to pray daily for our children, and grandchildren, as well as join our efforts to theirs in caring for all of them in general. Their own role in fulfilling God's injunction is to join others in the world to continue from where we, their parents and grandparents left off, just as we took over from our parents and grandparents. This is to ensure that God's purpose for procreation from one generation to another continues.

Staying With God Brings Prosperity

Considering the prosperity in our marital life, we are tempted to state that it is because we have never left the presence of God, and in our day-to-day activities hence, God himself has never abandoned us to stay in darkness or in want. That said, we know certainly that we have had our ups and downs in the years past. We have also been overwhelmed by our own weaknesses, as no human being is perfect. For instance, we quarrel virtually every day over little things such as not being ready in time for prayers or for Mass. This makes us grow stronger in faith, as our quarrels usually come with a positive push towards the development of our faith. This is one of our 'secrets' that is being revealed here in case some may wish to put this into practice. Just as we learnt a lot from Pope St John Paul II during the nearly twenty-seven years of his pontificate, Pope Francis has also been providing much through his Catechesis, to help us build up a strong faith in our marital relationship. From his encyclicals, we always have something to hold on to, that *fires* our spirit to take complete control of the situation in hand in order to move ahead, using every occasion to give thanks and praise to God, no matter how distressing the situation may be.

Sustaining Marriage With the Holy Eucharist

Those who are not Catholics may not easily understand the fact that our sacramental marriage can be well protected and sustained by the Holy Eucharist. This is another 'secret' that is being revealed by us today after forty-five years of marriage. The reason for revealing this is that people are fond of asking us questions such as: 'What are the ingredients for sustaining a sacramental marriage in the Catholic Church?'.

From what we have stated above without any ambiguity, many can take something home. It is our hope that those who are already in a marriage or who are planning to get married will learn something new as we continue this self-revealing story of our marital life. Our hope is that the reader will get something worthwhile out of this that can help him or her to sustain their marriage. We are doing this in the hope that those who are already married and doing well in their marriages can also contribute their own 'secrets' to what is being revealed here in this book.

Be that as it may, we wish to state that there are many ways in which properly conducted Christian marriages can be sustained by the couples themselves to enable their marriage to last 'until death do them part'.

Holding Dear the Grace of God

We are definitely sure that many married couples who are still very much in love with each other after forty years of marriage and still practising their faith will have many experiences to share with people, regarding the things that have helped them to sustain their own marriage.

What we can happily state from our own experience is that marriage is sustained mainly by the grace granted by God to the couple, and which the couple must hold dear by putting the following into practice:

(i) getting their family members together for regular family prayer, knowing very well that 'a family that prays together stays together', as pointed out by Fr Patrick Peyton and creditably used by St Teresa of Calcutta during her apostolic work

(ii) attending daily Masses, if possible, with their children and nourishing themselves spiritually with Holy Communion

(iii) practical expression of their love for each other in many ways, from loving kisses, hugging each other, sending each other birthday cards, etc.

(iv) satisfying each other sexually and avoiding sex when the other partner is not ready

(v) refusing to be lured outside the matrimonial home despite certain attractions and immoral activities going on in the world around us.

(vi) caring largely for the children whom God has blessed the couple with in terms of spiritual development and proper education in schools

(vii) spending holidays together away from home, and sometimes with children in a new environment

(viii) caring for their parents who brought them to life and their siblings, both spiritually and materially

(ix) renewing their vows of marriage at yearly marriage anniversaries

(x) buying and packaging special gifts for each other at unexpected times

(xi) giving good moral education to their children at home as both parents spend quality time together with them

(xii) paying the children's school fees on time and showing a keen interest in children's performances in schools

(xiii) providing for the upkeep of the home, with both parents playing their part as much as they can: the husband providing money for the food while the wife ensures that the food is prepared in good times

(xiv) ensuring that marriage anniversaries are celebrated as a Thanksgiving Day from the home to the Church, and with friends to share God's blessings

(xv) taking everyone through routine physical and mental exercises to ensure that everyone is in good stead, and quite ready to face the tasks ahead

(xvi) ensuring that there is no viewing of pornographic programmes and other scandalous materials on television, laptops or on other electronic gadgets at home

(xvii) teaching the children and other family members about the need to attend to the poor, the elderly and the stranger in our midst, etc.

More Testimonies Needed From People in Flourishing Christian Marriages

The list of positive things to do is endless and married couples can add more and more to it from their own experiences. What is quite sure is that these good gestures, coupled with agape love and good communication will make a good Christian marriage thrive in the face of difficulties.

It is also instructive to know that the attitude of giving selfless service keeps one's marriage blossoming in love, with both partners making themselves available regularly for the reception of the Holy Eucharist as well as being active participants in church activities. Our experiences in our marital life may be seen to be slightly different from what the reader may already have been told by others. What we can recommend here is to take what appeals to you from these experiences and add them to the positive ones you have learnt elsewhere, then apply conscious efforts to put them into practice.

The reader may learn in the process that what married couples do and take for granted in Africa may be seen as impracticable in Europe or in America because of the cultural background.

Uncommon Practices

This is why it may seem quite odd to learn that some things married couples in Europe or America do with ease and great enthusiasm in their countries are found to be uncommon in our African continent. This may include such things as public displays of love for one's wife such as opening the door of one's car for her to be seated before the man gets in his own seat and drives the car away. An African may see this as 'showmanship' and nothing more, since there are higher numbers of divorce cases among married couples in the western world than in married couples in Africa. In the same way, the African sees the issue of couples kissing each other profusely in public as corrupting the minds of the innocent. African society therefore takes this seriously, especially when they see the women involved in this act also dressing in such a way that they are casually exposing part of their thighs and/or breasts as they walk down the street. This, to the African, is unacceptable and should not be imitated.

So, no matter what one thinks about the cultural differences, and the response to such issues as kissing in public, some of the basic elements that help a great deal in sustaining marriage anywhere in the world are those mentioned above. As already indicated, there are many other good deeds that can be added to the list above, with regards to what one can do to sustain his or her marriage.

What we have just done here is attempt to remind each other, especially Catholics who are married or preparing to get married, what we all need to do to keep our marriages not only prosperous but also in line with God's plan so that we can enjoy our marriages while we are still alive.

Questions Challenging Us Daily

Having seen some of the things we can do daily to make our marriages enjoyable, many questions confronting us that emerge from the above reflection include the following:

(a) what major roles are our own families playing to ensure that God's purpose of creating human beings is fulfilled here on earth?

(b) are we bearing good children to help fill the earth?

(c) are we in the activities of promoting life or are we anti-life?

(d) do we support the initiatives to ensure that we have a conducive environment for human beings to live happily in or are we helping to destroy the environment by our actions to make it difficult for life to exist in our community or in some parts of the world?

(e) are we using contraceptives to limit the number of children being born as our own way of rejecting God's injunction, instructing humans to 'be fruitful, multiply and fill the earth'?

(f) are we connected with the use of weapons of mass destruction, be it automatic guns, explosives, dynamite, atomic bombs, nuclear missiles, chemical weapons, etc., that can destroy millions of people, animals, trees, vegetation, infrastructures, etc. and make the areas that are destroyed inhabitable?

(g) as married Catholics, what roles do we play in our Church and/or in our society that make our own marriage different from others, that would make people want to imitate ours?

(h) are we contributing meaningfully to the development of our Church and our society to make the world a better place for our children, grandchildren and the coming generations to live in?

(i) do we, in any way, indulge ourselves in corrupt practices in the office or in the marketplace in order to make life unbearable for others?

(j) can it be said that our family is devoted to prayers that could help our country and our people to come out of the woods in the face of its complex problems?

Solutions to Our Complex Problems

These are some of the salient questions that should agitate our minds as we gather in our domestic church to reflect on the current problems plaguing our society. It is only when we understand the unnecessary sufferings that these problems are creating in our marital life, and in our society at large that we can effectively commit them to prayers, imploring God to come to our aid. As we reflect on these issues in our domestic church, we should also be proffering solutions to these problems, because the world relies heavily on Catholics in power and the Catholic Church as a whole to show the light in all spheres of life, as regards the finding of solutions to our complex problems.

The solutions to both marital and societal problems should therefore emanate from our homes. Catholic and non-Catholic families alike must resolve, after discussing, the problems plaguing our society, to show impeccable conduct at home, in the Church, in the Mosque, in the marketplace, in the political arena, in places of work, in the government, etc.

Families to Be the Good News

Pope St John Paul II, who dwelt so much on families, and who, as indicated earlier in Volume One of this book, inspired me to begin my new apostolate, enjoined all families in the world, especially Christian families to be 'the Good News in the Third Millennium'. He believed rightly that Christian families have much to offer to the world in the area of the new evangelisation, beginning this evangelisation with their own families. Only recently, Pope Francis also called on all Christians, including married Catholic families, to see themselves 'as proclaimers of the resurrection of Jesus, not only in words, but also in the conduct and testimony of life', imploring all and sundry not to be docile witnesses but to be 'people who spread hope, with their way of welcoming, smiling and loving, above all loving because the power of the resurrection makes Christians capable of loving even when love seems to have lost its motivation'. This was part of the Pope's catechesis during his General Audience at St Peter's Square on Wednesday, 4 October 2017. His message was published on page three of *L'Osservatore Romano*, on 6 October 2017.

It must also be pointed out that the Archbishop of Benin City, Most Rev. Augustine Akubeze, who is currently the President of the Catholic Bishops' Conference of Nigeria (CBCN), has spent some time dwelling on what marriage should be for those who are in this institution established by God Himself, and how they can use this noble vocation to bring peace, prosperity and good political life to the nation.

Archbishop Augustine Akubeze's Proposal for Christian Marriage to Be a 'Mini-Heaven'

Archbishop Akubeze made this clear when he reflected on what the marriage institution is expected to be during the fiftieth wedding anniversary celebration of Rt. Hon. Damien and Dame Dr Esther Uduehi in Benin City.

At a Thanksgiving Mass attended by a number of Papal Knights and other special invitees from within and outside the country, he used the occasion of the wedding anniversary, which took place at St Paul's Catholic Church on 30 September 2017, to deliver part of his message to all married couples, with a view 'to encourage couples whose marriages are facing crisis, never to give up'.

He further told married couples to 'look for legitimate means to rectify and solve the problems you are facing. Once you know that there is no exit door in marriage you need to open up the doors of your life for the fresh wind of God to enter in through the power of the Holy Spirit and transform your bad situation into good', pointing out that 'God established marriage to be enjoyed'.

In conclusion he said: 'Do not allow your marriage to become a "mini-hell." It must become a "mini-heaven". We need to mention that for couples to enjoy their relationship and nurture it, they need to learn to value the other person. If you are in marriage, you need to truly let your spouse know that he or she is truly loved'.

A similar message was re-echoed by Fr Dr Victor Darlington, Parish Priest of Sacred Heart Church, Camberwell, London, UK, SE5 9QS, when he sent in the following piece:

What the Church Expects of a Catholic Marriage

Jesus Christ is the foundation of the domestic church. His invitation to everyone in the family especially to the young people intending to begin marital life is to know each other very well; and the engaged couple must be completely rooted and established in genuine friendship that can make love flourish.

Unfortunately, we often find that many young people end up marrying the wrong person. For marriage to truly flourish in a domestic church, couples must, first and foremost, be friends, who truly understand each other, their weaknesses and strengths and have also cultivated genuine willingness to accept their weaknesses as well. Marriage is 'for better, for worse; for richer, for poorer, in sickness and in health, until death'. This is what the Church expects of a Catholic marriage. There is no two-way about it.

The powerful words said by the engaged couple in the presence of an anointed priest of God or deacon and their sponsors are validly words of consent that make the marriage a sacrament. The moment you say these words to a wrong person, it marks the beginning of frustration and unhappiness. This is why the Church advises that even before engagement, couples must be sure they trust themselves and must be prepared for a life journey together because the Church will not grant any divorce for a marriage that has been validly conducted.

Sadly, many engaged couples do not spend much time to really understand each other and/or trust themselves as to what they are capable of doing to each other before bringing themselves up for marriage. This has, unfortunately led to the breakdown of some Christian marriages, especially when the couple later realised that either of them is the wrong person.

In such a situation, all hopes are still not lost as the unhappily married couples can seek advice from the Church and from psychologists on what to do to form a happy union or be separated and live their lives to the full as expected of good practising Christians. It is through such intervention that a way forward can be reached. It must be noted here that marriage is not meant for every person and people can live happily and practise their faith without necessarily going into marriage.

What is always important is to encourage our young intending couples to be vigilant. They need to be told over and over again before and during marriage classes, that those intending to present themselves for marriage must study themselves very well; know themselves in and out as best as they can humanly go, and avoid marrying a stranger instead of marrying a friend.

The Church therefore expects that when you present someone you love for marriage, both of you must have discovered that you are not only genuine friends, but also, you are both convinced beyond reasonable doubt that you already know each other well, both the good and the ugly. At the same time such couple presenting themselves for marriage is assuring the Church that both of them can lean on God as the foundation of their marital life, and stay happily together until death.

But it shows quite often that when you marry someone who is not a friend, he/she will always be hiding what could be described here as his or her 'passwords' to his/her iphone, computer and/or bank accounts. The end result of this is that a lot of lies and cheating of all forms will begin to rear their ugly heads, and these will make life unbearable for either party.

This definitely sends a good message that if you begin a relationship without friendship, it will, unfortunately, end in tears, for heaven helps those who help themselves. It is pointless to emphasise here that as we have many successful marriages today, so too we have a number of broken marriages, mostly due to bad choices and poor discernment.

In spite of what some people experience in marriage, it should be clear to all and sundry that marriage as designed by God is beautiful, prosperous and spirit-filled. Marriage is a sacrament that creates a domestic church. One can conclude this short contribution here by re-echoing the fact that it is advisable, healthier and more advantageous to wait a little longer to marry the right person than to make the mistake of hurrying to marry a wrong person.

May God continue to bless our young people with the wisdom and discernment they need to make the right choices in their lives.

With this contribution by Fr Dr Victor Darlington who is also a lecturer of Johaninne Studies at St John's Seminary, Wornesh Guildford, UK, on 'What the Church Expects of a Catholic Marriage', the curtain for this chapter is hereby lowered for the reader to make his or her reflections.

May God bless you and your families as you join in the crusade for promoting family spirituality as well as helping couples to sustain their marriages in our society.

Remember that the Holy Family Society has lined up a number of family formation programmes, specially designed for married couples, that can help them to sustain their individual marriages and make their domestic churches not only functional but also spiritually rewarding.

2

The Fundamentals for Running a Successful Domestic Church

We have, at the beginning of Chapter One, taken the reader through my reflection on my own marital life and how I have cooperated with my wife to carry out part of God's mandate to human beings: 'Be fruitful, multiply and fill the earth'. We have also seen how the Church expects us to conduct ourselves in our marriage in order to make it, in the words of Archbishop Augustine Akubeze, the President of the Catholic Bishops' Conference of Nigeria, a 'mini-heaven', instead of a 'mini-hell'.

Our main concern in this chapter therefore will be to put into perspective the fundamentals that will help families to live in perpetual peace by ensuring that their domestic churches thrive successfully as they take giant spiritual steps to advance their family spirituality and move towards holiness.

It should be noted here that when we speak of a Christian home in the Catholic Church, for instance, we are referring to a home where the husband and wife have had their baptism, confirmation and marriage celebrated in the Catholic Church, and are still practising according to the Catholic tradition. When a family is rooted in God, what is naturally experienced is that the children in the home will have a good upbringing and they become good models in society.

To ensure that the home is a good setting for evangelisation purposes, there are certain fundamentals parents must take along to successfully run a domestic church, especially when they have been blessed by God to have their own biological children, and are possibly also living with other family relations and wards. It is expected that parents who have conducted their marriages according to the Catholic tradition:

(a) remind themselves, from time to time, of the pledge they made on the day of their marriage, that they, as father and mother of the home, would bring up their children in the fear and love of God. This pledge they need to uphold to ensure that they formally bring up their children into the Catholic faith through infant baptism that washes away original sin. Thereafter, they are to prepare their children for the reception of the Holy Communion as they advance in age. This helps them greatly to build a home in Christ as they themselves advance in their marital life.

(b) recognise the fact that in their pursuits in life, the only way to come back to our Father who is in heaven is to maintain the struggle in life to meet their personal commitments to their family, to the church, to the community, and to the world at large, that at the end of their sojourn there will be nothing to prevent them from returning to the warm embrace of the Lord.

(c) learn and practice the act of charity. This is what Christ himself taught Simon Peter in John 21:15–17 by instructing him three times: 'Feed my lambs', 'Tend my sheep', and 'Feed my sheep'.

(d) bring to the understanding of everyone in the home that it is most spiritually rewarding to pray together as a family with hearts full of joy, following Christ's instruction indicating that: 'When you pray, you must not be like the hypocrites; ... go into your room and shut the door and pray to your Father who is in secret, and your Father who sees in secret will reward you' (Mt 6:5–6).

This being our guide, we must therefore take appropriate steps by ourselves to develop and sustain a functioning domestic church where we can commune with God on a daily basis. No one actually needs to be told about the importance of prayer because we have the good example from the twelve Apostles that, at a point in their own lives, they had to remove their hands from other duties in order to have quality time for prayers.

We learn from the scriptures that they had to select seven devoted members from among the disciples to be in charge of some duties they were previously engaged in, for them to have quality time to devote themselves 'to prayer and to the ministry of the word' (Acts 6:24). Apart from this, the bible is replete with the instances where our Lord Jesus Christ himself withdrew from the crowds to find quiet places up the hill to pray. We also have a good guide from one of our popular songs that says: 'Jesus started with prayer and ended with prayer'.

These are pointers that we should devote quality time to prayer in our domestic church, with a view to carrying everyone in the home along to God.

(e) bring to the knowledge of everyone that a functioning domestic church leads its members to know God more, love him more and serve him more.

(f) train their children and wards to be good Christians that can navigate their own way, even through areas where they experience some pain and difficulties in life, to get on to the 'narrow road' that leads to heaven. Such children from good homes who are prepared to face the thick and thin of life by staying steadfastly with the Lord are easily identifiable in public by their words and deeds. These go to show how such children truly love Christ, our Lord, who in John 14:21 says: 'He who has my commandments and keeps them, he it is who loves me; and he who loves me will be loved by my Father, and I will love and manifest myself to him'.

(g) should make great efforts to continuously serve and worship the living God, and struggle daily to model their lives after Jesus, Mary and Joseph, the Holy Family of Nazareth. All in the family must also understand that this is the only model family that the almighty God has given to us to imitate in the world. And it is quite assuring that as people do God's will here on earth by imitating and putting into practice the virtues of Jesus, Mary and Joseph, there is a heavenly reward as promised by Christ himself.

(h) are to understand and teach others that from the scripture, we all learn that we are to 'love the Lord, your God, with all your heart, and with all your soul and with all your might' (Deut 6:5; Mt 22:37). And that the same scripture instructs us all to 'love your neighbour as yourself' (Mt 22:39).

(i) who have more experiences of day-to-day living are to teach others in the family what their experiences in serving the living God have been, giving testimonies about their successes and encounters while serving the Lord. For instance, elders in the family could speak in such a gathering about their experiences in willingly opening wide their hands to welcome strangers into their homes, especially those who are stranded, since our Lord Jesus Christ reminds us every day that on the last day of Judgement he would say to us: 'I was a stranger and you welcomed me' (Mt 25:35).

(j) are to let others in the household know that the essence of being active participants in family devotion in the domestic church is to implore the almighty God to give everyone the 'courage to put away all malice and all guile and insincerity and envy and all slander' (1 Pt 2:1). That everyone is to come to God 'like newborn infants, long for the pure spiritual milk that by it, you may grow up to salvation; for you have tasted the kindness of the Lord' (1 Pt 2:2–3).

(k) should let all participants at the family devotion know that the main reason for setting up the domestic church is to have everyone praying together with a singular purpose, and with everyone consciously saying: 'one thing have I asked of the Lord; that will I seek after; that I may dwell in the house of the Lord all the days of my life, to behold the beauty of the Lord and to inquire in his temple, he will conceal me under the cover of his tent, he will set me high upon a rock' (Ps 27:4–5).

(l) should let everyone know that the continuous acquisition of material things to take precedence over having quality time to serve and worship God is very wrong and quite unhelpful in seeking God's favour. This means that in spite of our regularity at our domestic church, we must stop other businesses we are engaged with in order to have time to attend, and be an active participant at Mass, particularly on Sundays and on Holy Days of Obligation.

(m) should let all participants in the domestic church know that the aim of their struggles in life should be towards the continuous storage of our treasures in heaven through good works done here on earth. That no one therefore should concentrate on acquiring material things at the loss of his or her soul, since we all came naked and empty, and we will also return naked and empty after our earthly sojourn.

Active Participation in the Domestic Church Is to Be Followed by Good Works

If the married couple who oversee the goings on in the domestic church understand the above and teach them to their children, relations and wards, they will all grow up spiritually in faith and live in peace with one another. And for them to enjoy enduring peace in the home, their Christian faith must be backed up with good practice of what they learn from the scriptures, especially as they pertain to the carrying out of good works at home and in the community. This makes the individual members of a household become not only one another's keeper but also a model in the community. The carrying out of good works enriches the love for one another in a community, and such 'love covers a multitude of sins' (1 Pt 4:8).

In this type of setting, it will be seen by people that members of a household where the domestic church thrives have faithfully ascribed the correct meaning to the Christian message they receive daily or periodically during their prayer devotion and the sharing that takes place among themselves. What this further shows is that the participants in the daily family devotion are not only walking their way to holiness but are also moving swiftly to the narrow path, with a view to reaching the 'narrow gate'.

It is for this reason, to help everyone get to the narrow gate by employing some spiritual tools to help in forming its members that the Holy Family Society really came into existence. The spiritual tools help family members to appreciate God in all sincerity, thanking him every day for the favours bestowed on the individual members of the family. When properly used, these veritable, handy spiritual tools aid incisive, faith-building reflections, and help greatly to prepare one for a purposeful life in the community. This also explains the reason for adding three volumes of this book to the various works already produced by the society to promote its way of family spirituality.

The various works, as a good number of people have testified, also provide a great deal of assistance to families who want to create functioning domestic churches. Many who use the spiritual tools in their domestic churches have very encouraging testimonies to share with people as they confirm the good things that have happened in their individual families by sticking to the family spirituality programmes of the Holy Family Society.

From the reports so far received, the Holy Family Society, having made this one of its cardinal programmes, needs to be fully supported to prompt more Christians and non-Christians to buy into the project of turning their homes into domestic churches, knowing fully well that an eternal reward awaits those who do the Father's will here on earth. There is no doubting the fact that our engagements in our domestic church help greatly to build up our faith in God. When this is accompanied by purity of heart and an inclination to do good works at any given opportunity that one has, one finds visible progress not only in one's home but also in the society at large. This powerfully supports the idea of making the domestic church functional and relevant in our community.

Giving Out Your Best to Serve and Worship the Living God

Having known this, the Holy Family Society is anxious to spread this message to all and sundry and to welcome more members into its fold because we believe in opening wide our doors to many from different walks of life, Christians and non-Christians alike. Members of the society are expected to learn this themselves to enable them to have the opportunity of giving out the best of what the society has in stock to those who thirst for them. This is the only way to use and put into practice the fundamentals already identified above in their day-to-day engagements with members of the public.

By so doing, they will find themselves engaged in various spiritual functions, teaching people the Christian principles of good living, and at the same time serving the living God through others. This is certainly what the society has that it can give out to its active and associate members.

Be that as it may, the Holy Family Society wants all to know that there is no shortcut to holiness and it is not something one can buy with money, no matter how much money one has in his or her bank accounts in different parts of the world. The only way to holiness is to make personal sacrifices right from the comfort of one's home, giving quality time for prayers, just like the way the Apostles and early disciples of Christ did, and putting into practice all that one learns every day from the scriptures, from the tradition of our forefathers in faith and from the good aspects of our own culture. This, to our view, is the way to work towards holiness.

In advancing our family spirituality, the Holy Family Society believes that it is essential for its members as well as all Christians and non-Christians alike to adopt and put into practice the virtues of Jesus, Mary and Joseph as they struggle every day to live their individual lives. May our Lord Jesus Christ give us the wisdom to understand this fundamental truth.

What are these virtues, the inquisitive minds might want to ask here? They include: the virtues of agape love, patience, simplicity, humility, faithfulness, prayerfulness, dignity of labour, self-control, self-abandonment, thanksgiving, joyful celebration, etc. The practice of these virtues cuts across all religions. This is why the Holy Family Society is not restrictive in presenting its message to all and sundry.

Putting the Virtues of the Holy Family of Nazareth Into Practice
It is our belief that the practise of these virtues by Christians and non-Christians alike will help people, to a large extent, to up to holiness. The reason for focusing on this is that those who have so far been canonised as saints by the Catholic Church were, during their lifetime here on earth, members of their own individual families. There was no one among them who did not come from a particular family. Some are even known to have been believers of traditional religion before they were converted. This being the case, the road is clear for those who have the holy desire to pick up their crosses to follow in the footsteps of Jesus Christ in anticipation of their steadfastly climbing the ladder of holiness until they get to their real home in heaven.

All we can do henceforth is to continuously pray to the almighty God to grant us the wisdom to steer our course in this world to follow the path of life so that all our struggles in this life will not be in vain.

We should also continue to pray that families in the world would not allow the insurgence of coronavirus, which suddenly caused thousands of deaths in the world, or any other deadly virus/disease, to dissuade people from going back to the Church and/or prevent them from being on their ladder of holiness that will take them to heaven.

Conclusion

As we prepare members of our household to stick to and teach the fundamentals of promoting and sustaining the domestic churches, let us remember that our constant focus should always be on doing our best in this world so that at the end of time, we will be able to join those who 'do right and entrust their souls to a faithful Creator' (1 Pt 4:19). This is what we should all strive to achieve by our active participation in our Catholic Parish/Mass Centre programmes, in the programmes of pious societies in the Church, such as the spiritual programmes of the Holy Family Society; and as we devote quality time to pray individually and/or collectively in our domestic churches while worshipping almighty God.

If our intentions are pure as we consciously do this every day, almighty God himself will provide us with sufficient grace and the strength to overcome any obstacles on our way. This is the plain truth, and when God says 'yes', nobody can say 'no'. As we come to the end of our reflections here, we also need to move on, referring to the opinions of experts to determine 'What the Church Expects of a Functioning Domestic Church'. So, the following Chapters Three and Four of this volume will reflect the views of some of our Church leaders. Happy reading.

3
_____

Catholic Teaching About a Spirit-filled Domestic Church

By Most Reverend Emmanuel Adetoyese Badejo
Bishop, Catholic Diocese of Oyo

The importance of the mission that God intended for all families needs to be constantly re-stated and re-presented in our day. If the Church is, in simple terms, 'where two or three meet in my name' (Mt 18:20), then we all ought to be the church. This is why the efforts and purpose of Sir David Osunde, Founder and National Coordinator of the Holy Family Society, are so important, and deserving of the support and attention of all.

Of the Family, Marriage and Life

In Africa, respect for human life, marriage and family are the three proverbial *aaro meta ti kii da obe nu* (the three stones that keep the pot of soup securely on fire) tripod, which keeps human society from collapse. The family is the umbrella of all three. Life comes from God. We believe that marriage is ordered by God and he himself came into the world through a family. No other institution therefore predates the family as the place in which to reconnect the human being with the almighty God and grow wholesome values. Family, therefore, must be taken most seriously.

Life is God's gift because God is love. The union of man and woman brings about what is known as 'marriage' and the beginning of the human family. Therefore, the family is the cradle of everything good in human society. It is needless to emphasise here that no human being came into this world without a family, even though some may not have been accepted into their family due to the circumstances surrounding their birth. However, that does not mean they do not belong to a family.

Pope St John Paul II in his encyclical, *Familiaris Consortio*, no. 17, speaks extensively on this unique gift of marriage and family. In fact, the Compendium of the Social Doctrine of the Church (CSDC), declares in no. 225: 'The responsibility for protecting and promoting the family as a fundamental natural institution, precisely in consideration of its vital and essential aspects, falls to the whole of society'. The need to confer an institutional character on marriage, basing this in a public act that is socially and legally recognised, arises from the basic requirements of social nature. Confirmed, the family, as a domestic Church, has an indispensable role to play in the education of the members and for the good of the larger society.

In a paper that I presented in Angola for the Bishops of Africa at the level of the Symposium of Episcopal Conferences for Africa and Madagascar (SECAM) in 2012, I wrote the following:

> The family has consistently been described as the bedrock of society, until the advent of new ideologies. Sociologists Zinn and Eitzen (2002, P.7) referred to the family as 'a haven, a place of intimacy, love and trust'. Macionis (2011, P.112) described the family as 'an agent of socialization and the primary source of influence behind the formation of personality and the growth of a child.' In fact, the Church, has self-defined herself as family in Africa asserting that 'a man and a woman united in marriage, together with their children, form a family', 'a domestic church' (CCC 2202), and the original cell of social life'. It goes further to describe it as the 'community in which, from childhood, one can learn moral values, begin to honour God and make good use of freedom.

Family life is an initiation into life in society.' (CCC 2207, 2208).[1]

Challenges Facing the Family

The truth is that the enemies of the family take it more seriously than the rest of us. Today those forces that militate against the correct understanding of the family are numerous and powerful and they work much harder than those who ought to really care about the family. I wish to illustrate that point with a little story about the late reggae musician, Robert Nesta Marley. He had been shot and seriously wounded some three days before a major scheduled show. So many people concluded that he would not be able to make it. He surprised everyone by showing up and performing rather than cancelling the show. When asked why he took such a big risk, he said he had to because the agents of darkness were working without taking any rest. He felt that to have any chance against them, he as an agent of light had to take even greater risks and make all efforts possible. I list here some of the forces militating against the family in our time:

- A deliberate undermining of religion and faith in God so as to create a world without moral absolutes, thereby elevating subjectivism.

- A deliberate and massive campaign to repurpose, discredit and weaken Christian symbols, teachings and practice through:

  ◆ Massive media campaigns for artificial family planning being presented as the most normal and harmless thing ever. This is a lie!

---

[1] Bishop Emmanuel Adetoyese Badejo, 'The Influence of Modern Media and New Ideologies on the Family in Africa Today', Symposium of Episcopal Conferences for Africa and Madagascar, Angola, 2012.

- Lobbies by powerful, global governing bodies, NGOs and individuals with large funds against traditional African values.

- Offer of a false sense of freedom for the youth and women in contraception.

- Fearmongering, false messages and half-truths.

- Portrayal of the Church and the Gospel of Life as archaic and insensitive.

- Portrayal of African Culture as very insensitive and oppressive of women.

- Pervasive and indiscriminate introduction of so-called Comprehensive Sexuality Education (CSE) in all institutions of learning, thereby promoting the culture of death.

All these powerful influences are challenging established societal hierarchies, including religion and faith, and are forging new links between groups and peoples, often in subtle ways, making them rethink their ideas about family and family life, especially marriage, gender, sex, intimacy and the meaning of life and existence, to name a few.

The Family as a Domestic Church

The concept of the Christian Family as a domestic Church is neither a recent creation nor is it even conventional. Man cannot claim to be the originator of the family. That origin must be stretched back to the plan of the Almighty Creator for Adam and Eve when he said 'be fruitful and multiply' (Gn 1:22) and to all the families blessed by God in the old testament, including that of Abraham. When Abraham had to respond in obedience to God's commandment, he taught some catechism to Isaac, his son. Isaac, having been loaded with the wood for the burnt offering, asked his father: 'Here are the fire and the wood, but where is the lamb for the burnt offering?' (Gn 22:7). Abraham taught him to look up to God: 'My son, God himself will provide the lamb for the burnt offering' (Gn 22:8).

God eventually did provide the lamb and Isaac was saved. That lesson about trusting God in everything was taught by the father to his child. This is essentially what the family does, being the first place where people learn about God, to direct people to their Creator. Abraham did just that as leader of his version of the domestic church.

Psalm 128 expresses similar sentiments on how he who fears the Lord is blessed by having his wife and children like a fruitful vine round his table, and eventually seeing his children's children. The Church is where the fear of the Lord is taught to be a blessing. No other place other than the family can be synonymous with that experience.

From Adam and Eve through to Abraham, fast forward to God's greatest intervention in human history when he sent his only begotten son, Jesus, into the world so that all who believe in him might be saved (Jn 3:16). Jesus came into the world through the Holy Family. Joseph and Mary were the ones who introduced Jesus, in his humanity, into the temple and taught him the religious laws and practices of his time. They helped him to grow in the way of God as he was beholding to them. That was Jesus' domestic church. Through the Holy Family, God ordained all families for this divine purpose. The family is the ideal place for imbibing great values of love, tolerance, reconciliation, forgiveness, solidarity, equity and justice.

Nurturing and Securing the Domestic Church

The family, in order not to be swept off its feet by such domineering and often secular and negative influences, needs to be a domestic church. Such a domestic church would provide a platform where:

All its components regularly attend church. This will bring immeasurable benefits to the family and to the society at large. It has also been scientifically proven that irrespective of the religion people practice, the practice of religion does contribute to the stability of society. This gives the lie to the effort of people who would like to classify religion or church attendance as futile or ineffective engagements.

In her book entitled: *Stand for the Family,* Sharon Slater, President of Family Watch International, quotes Dr Patrick Fagan, a family scholar, who wrote in an article: 'Regular attendance at religious services is linked to healthy, stable family life, strong marriages, and well-behaved children. The practice of religion also leads to a reduction in the incidence of domestic abuse, crime, substance abuse, and addiction. In addition, religious practice leads to an increase in physical and mental health, longevity and education attainment. Moreover, these effects are intergenerational, as grandparents and parents pass on the benefits to the next generations'.[2]

Dr Fagan, having analysed different studies that show the benefit of religion to the family concluded that religious beliefs and practices are connected with the following, among other things:

- Higher level of marital happiness and stability

- Stronger parent-child relationship

- Higher levels of self-control, self-esteem, and coping skills

- Higher levels of community cohesion and social support for those in need

- Lower levels of teen sexual activity

- Less abuse of alcohol and drugs

- Lower rates of suicide, depression and suicide ideation

---

[2] Sharon Slater, *Stand for the Family*, Family Watch International, 2010, p. 254; Dr Patrick Fagan, *The Heritage Foundation*, 'Why Religion Matters Even More: The Impact of Religious Practice on Social Stability', https://www.heritage.org/civil-society/report/why-religion-matters-even-more-the-impact-religious-practice-social-stability; accessed on 22 November 2021.

And many other such benefits. Clearly any family that can pass on these indices will rate well as a domestic church.

A domestic church will also be a platform where faith and ecclesiastical feasts, events and rituals like baptism, first holy communion, confirmation and marriages are joyfully appreciated, commemorated and celebrated. It would be a place where all should know about and have deference to resources like:

- Sacred Scripture
- The Catechism of the Catholic Church, which is the statement of the essential creed of the people of God
- The Documents of Vatican II
- The Compendium of the Church's Social Teachings
- The teachings of the Popes on the family

Such a domestic church will also be a place where all will have active roles to play in the life of the Church, as choristers, prayer leaders, Church wardens, altar servers, legionaries, etc.

Last but not least, a domestic church will also be a platform where clergy, religious and other pastoral agents are seen and treated with respect and are always made welcome.

What Then Really Makes the Family a Domestic Church?
In order to be considered an authentic domestic church, the family must be a small, basic community of believers capable of:

> Gathering around the Word of God and sharing it
> Living as a place of witness to solidarity, reconciliation and unity
> Proclaiming the message of Christ with their daily lives

The Church is comprised of various biological families and each family has a unique character that the child inherits through faith transmission and formation. This helps the child to lean on the faith and aspirations of the parents to grow spiritually or otherwise, which clearly shows that the education and faith formation of the child is an important element in family formation. Hence, for the child to understand the important aspects of what makes life special and in order to be fully integrated into the larger Church and society, proper family catechesis ought to take place such as:

- **Faith formation in the following areas:**
    - Catechesis/knowledge about the presence of the Supreme Being
    - Catechesis/initiation into the life of prayer and the meaning of prayer
    - Catechesis on the sanctity and preservation of life

- **Since the family is fundamentally enriched to welcome and nourish lives, a domestic church is expected to:**
    - Promote faith, life's values and morals
    - Encourage a moral standard of living
    - Preparation for the easy absorption of members into the Ecclesial family that the larger Church builds on as ongoing formation
    - Share each other's burdens and joys, strengthen the relationship between parents and children

Concluding Thoughts

In conclusion, in today's world in which families are having serious challenges ranging from the culture of death, especially same sex unions, the craze for financial prosperity at all cost, inhumane acts such as human trafficking, prostitution, rape, cultural imperialism, lack of respect for values and morals leading to lack of peace, education decadence, lack of proper understanding of marriage and family, secularism and many others, the Christian family is indispensable. The human family has the great responsibility to be the good educator and a sign of hope in the way God has created it to be. Every Christian family should always remember 1 Corinthians 13:1 and 1 John 4:7–8, which call our attention to *love*.

It is heartwarming to note that cultures and faiths across the world still generally work to protect marriage and therefore, the family. The Bahai faith calls marriage a fortress for well-being and salvation where the man and woman are expected to be faithful to one another and considers childbearing a sacred obligation. Such convergence of thoughts and beliefs must serve to strengthen our will to promote the domestic church in the form that makes it remain a blessing to both humanity and contemporary society.

To families that are struggling to be faithful to their responsibilities despite the challenges of life, may God continue to be their strength. To families that are far away from the truth, may God bring them back to himself, and to the confused, may God enlighten their path to him. Amen.

4
_____

What the Church Expects of a Functioning Domestic Church

By Agbonkhianmeghe E. Orobator SJ
(President of the Jesuit Conference of Africa and Madagascar)

'The home of Nazareth is the school where we begin to understand the life of Jesus the school of the Gospel ... Here, in this school, one learns why it is necessary to have a spiritual rule of life, if one wishes to follow the teaching of the Gospel and become a disciple of Christ'
– Pope Paul VI, *Address in Nazareth*, 1964

Introduction: The Biblical and Historical Roots of the Domestic Church

These profound words of Pope Paul VI provide the context for understanding the vital significance of the domestic church in the life of the Church in the world. In keeping with the pope's understanding, the notion of a domestic church originates and is grounded in 'the home of Nazareth', that is, in the hearth and home of the Holy Family of Jesus, Mary and Joseph.

The notion of a domestic church has deep biblical and historical roots in the Church. It can be traced to the early Christian communities. In fact, the Church as an institution has its origins in domestic churches. Long before churches became physical edifices and locations set apart from the ordinary space of Christian life in society, the Church existed and functioned in clearly discernible domestic settings. It was a community of people at the heart of the family. The inventory of narratives and references to home churches in the early New Testament communities is quite impressive and fascinating, as are some of their characteristics.

In the first place, the home churches of the New Testament Christians were connected with particular people: parents, couples, community leaders and co-workers of the Apostles and disciples of Jesus Christ. In his letters, the apostle, Paul, always greets them and their domestic churches with reverence and affection.

Secondly, it is interesting that there was hardly any distinction between home churches presided over by women and those presided over by men.

Both men and women were active as believers, hosts, leaders and presiders in home churches. These churches were associated with a range of biblical personalities, like Mary of Jerusalem, the mother of John Mark (Acts 12:12); Lydia (Acts 16:40); Prisca and Aquila (Rm 16:3, 5; 1 Cor 16:19); Nympha (Col 4:15); and Philemon and Apphia (Phm 1–2). It is quite conceivable that other home or house churches existed that are not mentioned in the New Testament epistles.

Thirdly, the churches were inclusive of people beyond the immediate family. The fact that they were called home, house or domestic churches did not limit participation and membership to immediate family members only. In the real sense of the term, a home or house church was a place of gathering, a space where the church in its diversity gathered in prayer, praise and worship around the Word and the Eucharist.

Fourth, these churches were predominantly egalitarian communities. This is hardly surprising, giving that, in the early Christian communities, hierarchy to the extent that it existed was oriented primarily towards humble service rather than self-aggrandisement, status and privileges. From the names and personalities mentioned above who hosted churches in their homes, practically all of them were working lay women and men.

In the post-resurrection community of Luke-Acts, while the disciples and converts continued to worship in synagogues, they also 'devoted themselves to meeting together in the temple area and to breaking bread in their homes' (Acts 2:46). It is instructive that this central sacramental and eucharistic action of the community of the risen Christ took place in homes.

This fact suggests that in our times a functioning domestic church should be like the home churches of the early Christian communities. A domestic church provides a space where the Word is heard and shared and bread is broken, not in a sacramental sense, but in the offering of thanksgiving to God as a family. The domestic church should be a place of prayer. In this manner, the domestic church becomes a means for enriching, supporting, and deepening the faith of every member of the family.

The Domestic Church in African Theology

The importance of the domestic church has been recognised in African theology, in particular during the Special Assembly for Africa of the Synod of Bishops (aka The African Synod) in 1994. Alongside the African Synod, several important church documents link the domestic church with the institution of the family. This link is neither accidental nor specious. In reality, a functioning Christian family is the equivalent of a functioning domestic church.

In his post-synodal Apostolic Exhortation, *Ecclesia in Africa* (1995), Pope St John Paul II stated: 'In Africa in particular, the family is the foundation on which the social edifice is built. This is why the Synod considered the evangelisation of the African family a major priority, if the family is to assume in its turn the role of *active subject* in view of the evangelisation of families through families'.[1] By this statement, Pope St John Paul II recognised the family as the foundation of society. As such, the family plays an indispensable role

---

[1] Pope John Paul II, Post-Synodal Apostolic Exhortation *Ecclesia in Africa*, 80, Vatican, 1995.

in ensuring the proper functioning of society. The family has a missionary identity and function, as Pope St John Paul II further stated:

> The family has vital and organic links with society, since it is its foundation and nourishes it continually through its role of service to life: it is from the family that citizens come to birth and it is within the family that they find the first school of the social virtues that are the animating principle of the existence and development of society itself. Thus, far from being closed in on itself, the family is by nature and vocation open to other families and to society, and undertakes its social role.[2]

Based on this understanding, the African Synod adopted the theological model of 'Church as the Family of God'. This model or image of the Church is founded on the view that the family is not only a social unit, but also, more significantly, it is a domestic church: 'Along these lines, the Special Assembly for Africa affirmed that the goal of evangelisation is to build up the Church as the Family of God, an anticipation on earth, though imperfect, of the Kingdom. The Christian families of Africa will thus become true "domestic churches", contributing to society's progress towards a more fraternal life. This is how African societies will be transformed through the Gospel!'.[3]

As is evident in the foregoing, the theological and ecclesiological equivalence between 'Christian families of Africa' and true 'domestic churches' is indisputable. To reiterate a point already made above, a functioning family is a functioning domestic church. The African Synod further identified the extensive range of expectations of a functioning domestic church:

---

[2] Pope John Paul II, *Ecclesia in Africa*, 85.
[3] Pope John Paul II, *Ecclesia in Africa*, 85.

The Synod launched an explicit appeal for each African Christian family to become 'a privileged place for evangelical witness', a true 'domestic church', a community which believes and evangelises, a community in dialogue with God and generously open to the service of humanity.

'It is in the heart of the family that parents are by word and example ... the first heralds of the faith with regard to their children'. 'It is here that the father of the family, the mother, children, and all members of the family exercise the *priesthood of the baptised* in a privileged way "by the reception of the sacraments, prayer and thanksgiving, the witness of a holy life and self-denial and active charity". Thus the home is the first school of Christian life and "a school for human enrichment"'.[4]

The scope of the above declaration reveals in detail what the Church expects of a functioning domestic church. It recalls in part the practice of the early Christian communities as home and house churches. We see here clear and strong references to evangelisation, prayer, the 'priestly' role of parents and the formation of the younger members of the family in the faith of the Church and in Christian charity. On this last point, the African Synod insists on the role of parents: 'Parents are to see to the Christian education of their children. With the practical help offered by strong, serene and committed Christian families, Dioceses will develop a programme for the family apostolate as part of their overall pastoral plan'.[5]

In addition to the foregoing considerations, I would like to underscore two key expectations of the Church in regard to a functioning domestic church.

---

[4] Pope John Paul II, *Ecclesia in Africa*, 92.
[5] Pope John Paul II, *Ecclesia in Africa*, 92.

A Missionary Church

Far from confining its attention to local needs, the domestic church is a missionary church. Stated differently, the domestic church is mission-oriented. In the theological vision of Pope Francis, like the Universal Church, the domestic church is neither a self-focused nor an inward-looking institution. Its primary objective is not self-preservation. To become self-absorbed is to succumb to a narrow vision of the evangelising mission of the Church.

As Pope Francis wrote to the Argentine bishops shortly after his papal election, a self-referential church 'sickens from the stale air of closed rooms ... only looking to and relying on itself'. Accordingly, the pope would argue, a functioning domestic church is called to go forth. The domestic church is a church that goes forth and concerns itself with the needs of the larger society. This has several implications. In the first place, it means that every member of the domestic church is called to be a missionary: in virtue of their baptism, all the members of the People of God have become missionary disciples (cf. Mt 28:19). 'All the baptised, whatever their position in the Church or their level of instruction in the faith, are agents of evangelisation'.[6]

Secondly, this same expectation applies to the domestic church, because 'The Church is herself a missionary disciple'.[7] In particular, the domestic church is a church that reaches out to the existential peripheries in order to attend to the needs of the poor, the marginalised, persons with disabilities, and the oppressed. 'Each Christian and every community must discern the path that the Lord points out, but all of us are asked to obey his call to go forth from our own comfort zone in order to reach all the "peripheries" in need of the light of the Gospel'.[8]

---

[6] Pope Francis, Apostolic Exhortation *Evangelii Gaudium*, 120, Vatican, 2013.
[7] Pope Francis, *Evangelii Gaudium*, 40.
[8] Pope Francis, *Evangelii Gaudium*, 20.

Another way in which Pope Francis describes a mission-oriented church is the church as a 'field hospital' – one that is committed to the mission of healing, reconciliation and mercy.

In his Angelus address on 20 September 2020, Pope Francis summarised the meaning, importance and risks of a mission-oriented Church:

> Our communities are also called to go out to the various types of 'boundaries' there might be, to offer everyone the word of salvation that Jesus came to bring. It means being open to horizons in life that offer hope to those stationed on the existential peripheries, who have not yet experienced, or have lost, the strength and the light that comes with meeting Christ. The Church needs to be like God: always going out; and when the Church does not go out, it becomes sick with the many evils we have in the Church. And why are these illnesses in the Church? Because she does not go out. It is true that when someone goes out there is the danger of getting into an accident. But it is better a Church that gets into accidents because it goes out to proclaim the Gospel, than a Church that is sick because it stays in. God always goes out because He is a Father, because He loves. The Church must do the same: always go out.[9]

Francis's compelling summary reiterates what he stated forcefully in *Evangelii Gaudium* (no. 49):

> I prefer a Church which is bruised, hurting and dirty because it has been out on the streets, rather than a Church which is unhealthy from being confined and from clinging to its own security. I do not want a Church concerned with being at the centre and which then ends by being caught up in a web of

---

[9] Pope Francis, *Angelus* on 20 September 2020, Vatican, 2020.

obsessions and procedures. If something should rightly disturb us and trouble our consciences, it is the fact that so many of our brothers and sisters are living without the strength, light and consolation born of friendship with Jesus Christ, without a community of faith to support them, without meaning and a goal in life. More than my fear of going astray, my hope is that we will be moved by the fear of remaining shut up within structures which give us a false sense of security, within rules which make us harsh judges, within habits which make us feel safe, while at our door people are starving and Jesus does not tire of saying to us: 'Give them something to eat' (Mk 6:37).

Based on Pope Francis's ecclesial vision, a functioning domestic church loses its identity if it fails to become the light of the gospel both in the family and in society. Again, the domestic church is a church that goes forth. The African Synod has mentioned a similar expectation of a functioning domestic church: 'The Christian family, as a "domestic Church" built on the solid cultural pillars and noble values of the African tradition of the family, is called upon to be a powerful nucleus of Christian witness in a society undergoing rapid and profound changes'.[10]

A Safe and Nurturing Church

The idea of house churches and the sacramental eucharistic and baptismal experiences within them attested to in the New Testament offers us a useful model for envisaging an ecclesial arrangement that includes the child as a valued and honoured member of the body of Christ. Added to this is the phenomenon of mass (family) conversions in the early churches. As mentioned, the New Testament widely attests to this phenomenon in the apostolic era. There is no doubt that as a theological experience, both writers and eyewitnesses focus on the adult experiences – questions that are asked, actions

---

[10] Pope John Paul II, *Ecclesia in Africa*, 92.

performed, and teachings proclaimed. Reference to children is either rare or non-existent.

As we now know, unfortunately, despite its well-attested values, like the Church, the family is not the safest place for children. Research has shown that a higher percentage of sexual abuse of children and minors occurs in homes and in family settings. These abuses are perpetrated by people known to the victims. This fact does not mitigate the egregious nature of the sexual abuse of minors and vulnerable people in the Church. In reality, these abuses harm the family and the Church.

In his Apostolic Letter issued *Motu Propio*, *Vos Estis Lux Mundi* (7 May 2019), Pope Francis declared that abuses of whatever kind committed against minors and vulnerable people inflict 'physical, psychological and spiritual damage to the victims and harm the community of the faithful'. He insisted that to ensure that such phenomena 'never happen again, a continuous and profound conversion of hearts is needed, attested by concrete and effective actions that involve everyone in the Church, so that personal sanctity and moral commitment can contribute to promoting the full credibility of the Gospel message and the effectiveness of the Church's mission'.

Francis' call echoed his previous declaration that 'no effort must be spared to create a culture able to prevent such situations from happening, but also to prevent the possibility of their being covered up and perpetuated. The pain of the victims and their families is also our pain, and so it is urgent that we once more reaffirm our commitment to ensure the protection of minors and of vulnerable adults'.[11] In sum, the abuse of children damages the family and the Church.

In this context, a functioning domestic church should be a safe bastion against any attitude, practice or behaviour that could endanger or violate the dignity and integrity of the child. A

---

[11] Pope Francis, *Letter of His Holiness Pope Francis to the People of God*, Vatican, 2018.

functioning domestic church should provide a safe, nurturing and healthy environment for children to learn, grow and flourish. As Pope Francis has also declared, 'The Church loves all her children like a loving mother, but cares for all and protects with a special affection those who are smallest and defenceless. This is the duty that Christ himself entrusted to the entire Christian community as a whole. Aware of this, the Church is especially vigilant in protecting children and vulnerable adults'.[12] This is a clear mandate on how a functioning domestic church should fulfil its missionary vocation.

Conclusion

The notion of a domestic church is rooted in the history, tradition and scriptures of the Church. The Church in Africa and the Universal Church have outlined what is expected of a functioning domestic church. As detailed above, these expectations required the full commitment of all family members, beginning with parents. A functioning domestic church is a vibrant witness to and proclaimer of the Gospel of Jesus Christ and a catalyst for the evangelisation and transformation of the family and the world.

---

[12] Pope Francis, Apostolic Letter issued *Motu Propio, As a Loving Mother*, Vatican, 2016.

5

Domestic Church: Experiences From the World Meeting of Families in Philadelphia

All who have been regular participants at the World Meeting of Families will testify that there is always a lot to take home at the end of every one of these Vatican sponsored, triennial family meetings meant to help families develop their domestic churches and promote the new evangelisation mission throughout the world.

The spiritual gains from the World Meeting of Families are expected to be used profitably by active participants not only to improve their own family spirituality, but also to make their domestic churches much more functional and beneficial to others who are desirous of improving their own spirituality. It is for this reason that I wish to make known here some of the lessons I learned personally from the Eighth World Meeting of Families held in Philadelphia, USA in 2015, which I joyfully shared with others as soon as I arrived back to my country.

During the five-day meeting, the whole world was seemingly gripped with love, a genuine love for all God's creation. This was what thousands of the participants felt and took home as one of the essential ingredients of peaceful living. It was undoubtedly great fun and a period of sharing the genuine love anchored in our Christian faith with others from different parts of the world. The gathering was quite unique in every sense of the word, as thousands of pilgrims gathered in the 'City of Brotherly Love' as Philadelphia is referred to in America. Most Christians and non-Christians in the world, including the self-proclaimed atheists, were touched by the all-consuming *divine love* that filled the hearts of participants during the huge international event. It was an overwhelming love that was meant to be shared with the whole world. So, whatever we received in terms of this genuine love was subsequently shared through social, electronic and print media as well as through interpersonal contact with families in our immediate neighbourhoods.

This gave the opportunity to millions of families to experience this enduring, world-changing love that has been freely given to us as a special gift of God. Many people seemed to have forgotten that this is a free gift from God, and for no just reason have not been able to share this freely with the people they interact with in their daily activities. The Vatican had taken the initiative to remind everyone about this overwhelming genuine love that God has shared with us but which we find difficult to share with others.

It should be noted here that all the participants were prepared to learn more about this as the Holy Father, Pope Francis, through the instrumentality of the Pontifical Council for the Family, had sufficiently tapped from the 'light of love' in the horizon to set the theme of the international event. It was because of this that he earlier announced, a few months before the events through the Vatican information network, the theme for the Eighth World Meeting of Families, appropriately titled, 'Love is Our Mission: The Family Fully Alive'. The theme captured the real mission of the Church and that of the domestic church, both of which are fully aware of their innate responsibility in the area of spreading authentic love in the family and throughout the entire world.

Those who had followed this unquenchable light of love in the horizon, which the World Meeting of Families evoked from its last station in Milan, Italy, in 2012, to Philadelphia in 2015, were quite anxious to see it settle down naturally once more in this City of Brotherly Love for the whole world to learn a new lesson on love. The

Vatican's plan was to prompt everyone to genuinely appreciate, respect and love everything in the world, just as God expected Adam and Eve to love and eat of anything in the Garden of Eden, except the forbidden fruit.

The Garden of Eden, the Church has constantly reminded us, represents the whole world, which Pope Francis also describes as our common home. The only thing that can make any of us recognise all that is contained in the world is the light of love, which penetrates through all impediments to illuminate the hearts of those who give themselves freely to God. It is this same light of love that helps those who yearn for the things of God to see clearly the 'forbidden fruits' in the world.

Each person was intended to reflect on how God 'took man and put him in the Garden of Eden to till it and keep it. And the Lord God commanded the man, saying, "You may freely eat of every tree of the garden; but of the tree of knowledge of good and evil you shall not eat, for in the day you eat of it you shall die"' (Gn 2:15–17). Alas! The serpent deceived the woman and the woman ate of the fruit and gave a part to the man who also ate of the forbidden fruit because the serpent had deceived the woman, saying, 'you will not die. For God knows that when you eat of it, your eyes will be opened and you will be like God, knowing good and evil' (Gn 3:4–5).

The Vatican wanted the participants to reflect deeply on how sin entered the world and how family members can strive always to avoid occasions of sins in their daily activities, before the World Meeting of Families was officially opened on the 22 September 2015.

To ensure that people participated actively and freely in the scheduled events in Philadelphia and to ensure that there were no security breaches despite the high level of military preparations, Americans were solidly behind their government to forestall any evil plan. And for more than a year before the events, the Americans, whom people thought not to believe in prayer anymore because their government seemed to have ruled out the recitation of prayers in schools, began to recite daily specially composed prayers for the Pope and those who would participate in the event. One of these prayers is reprinted here below:

Prayer to St Michael for the Visit of Pope Francis

Saint Michael the Archangel, Defender of God's people, come to the assistance of His faithful, against whom the Powers of hell are unchained. Guard with special care our Holy Father, Pope Francis, on his pilgrimage to the United States. Saint Michael, bring the angels of Heaven to guide our streets and guide our hearts. Intercede for us with the Father that we may be a nation eager to listen, to learn and to grow in faith. May Pope Francis and his example of love and peace inspire us now and always, we ask this through Jesus Christ our Lord, Amen.

From the prayer above, one can state that the Americans still believe in God and the efficacy of prayers. Otherwise, they would have by now dropped their motto: 'In God We Trust'.

Be that as it may, most Americans, just like millions of others in the world, believe the scriptural story narrated about the Garden of Eden and how it was inhabited only by Adam and Eve, who were told not to eat the forbidden fruit as indicated above. But when they disobeyed God and ate the forbidden fruit, they saw themselves naked because sin had entered into them. As a result of this, their offspring were to suffer before they could eat. It was therefore not surprising that through Cain, one of their offspring, other forbidden fruits were sown throughout the world, the fruits of hatred, jealousy, murder, etc.

As the offspring of our early parents multiplied, more and more forbidden fruits were consciously sown in the world. In order to redirect the people back to himself, our ever-loving God sent his only beloved Son, Jesus Christ, to the world to redeem everyone. Only a few listened to him but those who did not like his message conspired to put him to death, death on the cross. From the scriptures, we all have learnt how 'the chief priest and the whole council sought false testimony against Jesus that they might put him to death' (Mt 26:59).

The same piece of scripture reveals that Pilate did not want to deal conclusively with the matter the chief priests and the whole council had brought before him. So, he washed off his hands saying, '"I am innocent of this righteous man's blood; see to it yourselves". And all the people answered, "His blood be upon us and our children"' (Mt 27:24–25). Jesus was eventually crucified and died a shameful death on the cross.

This explains why more and more forbidden fruits are still being continuously sown virtually every day in our world. These include ritual murder, kidnapping, human trafficking, greed, avarice, lust, different forms of scandal, religious bigotry, deceit, internet hacking, cyber fraud, drug trafficking, corruption, self-aggrandisement, and so forth. It is because all these have eaten deep into our society that the Church, in her wisdom, embarked on a new evangelisation scheme meant to redirect all families in the world to the great light of love in the horizon, which is hovering around the entire universe. This was why Pope St John Paul II, during his twenty-seven years of Pontificate, commissioned the World Meeting of Families.

As indicated earlier, the meeting held in Philadelphia, USA was the eighth edition, and it saw the whole world gripped with love as people watched Pope Francis presiding at some of the scheduled events. It was certainly another ample opportunity for all to reflect fruitfully on God's creation, focusing more on the good fruits that we see every day in this, our new Garden of Eden. These include children, youths, married men and women, persons with disabilities, persons from different cultural backgrounds, people with different vocations, people with different sexual orientation, people with different status in life, the environment, etc.

To take the participants through scriptural routes regarding the subjects lined up for the events, Church leaders and experts in various disciplines from different parts of the world were selected to lead discussions on numerous topics, beginning with a keynote address given on 22 September 2015, by Bishop Robert Barron, titled 'Living as the Image of God: Created for and Joy and Love'. This was essentially meant to explore the extravagant biblical claim that human beings have been made in the image and likeness of God, knowing well that 'Our likeness to God is revealed in our intelligence, our hunger for the good, our creativity, our freedom and above all in our capacity for relationship'.

From 23–25 September 2015, other keynote addresses that were given include the following:

23 September 2015

- 'The Light of the Family in a Dark World' by Cardinal Robert Sarah
- 'The School of the Heart: Parents as Primary Catechists' by Archbishop J. Michael Miller, CSB
- 'Saintly Couples: Models on the Road to Sanctity' by Mr Christian and Mrs Christine Meert
- 'Mary of Nazareth: The First Disciple and Mother of the Redeemer' by Deacon Harold Burke-Sivers
- 'Can Society Exist Without the Family?' by Dr Yves Semen
- 'Procreation as Co-creation: The Spirituality of Parenting' by Dr Joseph Atkinson, Mrs Nancy Atkinson, and Mrs Jennifer Anne Bissex (nee Atkinson)
- 'One Ring to Rule Them All: The Covenant of Marriage' by Archbishop Socrates B. Villegas
- 'Digging Into Dignity: Promoting the Dignity of the Human Person' by Prof. Teresa Stanton Collett
- 'The Bible: A Book for the Family; A Light for the World' by Fr Jean-Baptiste Edart, Mr Jorge Mario Quiceno Nieto, Mrs Duber Astrid Zabala Vera, and Ms Mary Elizabeth Sperry
- 'Creating the Future: The Fertility of Christian Love' by Prof. Helen Alvare

- 'Caring for Creation: Pope Francis and Environmental Stewardship' by Cardinal Peter Kodwo Appiah Turkson
- 'Rebuild My Church ... and Start From the Foundation: Living as "Domestic Church"' by Dr Timothy T. O'Donnell
- 'Family – Domestic Church: Way of Evangelisation and Ecumenism' by Msgr Renzo Bonneti, Rev. Nicky Lee, Mrs Sila Lee, Dr Alessandro Sona and Rev. Tory Baucum

24 September 2015

- 'A Gift From God: The Meaning of Human Sexuality' by Dr Juan Francisco de la Guardia Brin and Mrs Gabriela N. de la Guardia
- 'Ahead of Its Time: The Prophetic Character of Humanae Vitae' by Dr Janet Smith
- 'Free to Be Faithful? Religious Freedom and the Family' by Mrs Lucia Baez Luzondo
- 'The Holy Family and the Holiness of the Family' by Dr Andrew W. Lichtenwainer
- 'Creating a Flourishing Marriage Culture' by Prof. Robert P. George and Mr Sherif Girgis
- 'Living Through the Generations: Grandparents and Great Grandparents' by Mrs Catherine Wiley, Mr Philip Butcher, and Mr Michael La Corte
- 'The Family: A Home for the Wounded Heart' by Cardinal Luis Antonio Gokim Tagle
- 'The Sacred Balancing Act: Busy Lives and Family Spirituality' by Mrs Kathy Hendricks, Sr Patricia M. McCormack, IHM, Mr Damon Owens, and Mr Matthew Pinto
- 'Desiring Infinite Love: Sexuality in the Divine Plan' by Mr Christopher West

25 September 2015

- 'The Joy of the Gospel of Life' by Cardinal Sean Patrick O'Malley, OFM Cap. and Pastor Rick Warren
- 'Family Ties: How Meals, Rituals, Traditions, Worship and Prayers Create Strong Healthy and Joy-filled Catholic Families' by Mrs Lacy Rabideau
- 'Mom and Dad as the First Teacher of the Faith: Passing on the Faith to Your Children From Infancy to Adulthood' by Dr Rebecca Vitz Cherico
- 'The Way of the Cross, the Way of the Heart: Suffering and the Family' by Patriarch Fouad B. Twal, HB and Dr Salvatore Martinez

The purpose of listing the above topics and others that are not listed here because of space, is to show that at the triennial World Meeting of Families, the participants are always fully engaged to learn something new that they can take home for continued family spirituality development in their domestic church.

Along with the thought-provoking and enlightening keynote addresses that are listed above, there were altogether over 130 breakout session speakers on different topics. The participants were quite thrilled to listen directly to the speakers who are internationally recognised for their candid Christian views on marriage.

Since all the speakers are people of great wisdom and authority in their own rights, participants at the Eighth World Meeting of Families had ample choice of whom to listen to during the different sessions planned for each day, as the selected speakers were speaking on various topics at the same time but at different halls in the massive international Convention Centre at Broad Street Atrium in Philadelphia.

While this Adult Congress was going on, the Youth Congress was also being held in different halls in the expansive Convention Centre. These facilities enabled parents to leave their children to be cared for spiritually at the Youth Congress. I myself profited from this arrangement as I was there with twelve members of my family. It was certainly a profitable experience even for our seven grandchildren in the midst because the organisers cared for everyone's spiritual needs.

I was able to learn a lot from many of the experts who dwelt on issues relating to my family apostolate as well as the development of our domestic church. The session speakers who warmed my heart included Archbishop J. Michael Miller, OSB who presented a spirit-filled paper, 'The School of the Heart: Parents as Primary Catechists'. The summary of his paper as indicated in the circulated brochure is: 'Parents are the primary catechists of their children. Because of their baptism and the grace of marriage, they are equipped to fulfil the mission of handing down the faith to their children. A mother and father's witness of faithful love establishes their domestic church which is a school of virtue for the family'.

My wife and I were really enthused by this because it was this issue of handing down the faith to our children and grandchildren that propelled us to go with them to Philadelphia. Another speaker that took our attention on the second day of the congress was Deacon Harold Burke-Sivers. This was precisely because he had been seen frequently by viewers of Eternal World Television Network (EWTN) and so he was and is still well known for the energy with which he delivers his addresses. It was therefore not surprising when people trooped down to Terrace Ballroom III to hear him speak on 'Mary of Nazareth: The First Disciple and Mother of the Redeemer'. He explored the absolute awesomeness of the Blessed Virgin Mary and showed how 'her faith-filled "Yes" to becoming the Mother of God has over centuries drawn families into the life-giving communion with her son'.

There was also another prominent expert who addressed us on the second day of the congress. This was Dr Scott Hahn, who is also a regular guest speaker on EWTN. His topic was 'Back to the Garden of Eden: Unearthing God's Covenant with Humankind'. In his introduction to the spiritual talk, Dr Hahn directed the participants' attention to the scriptural passage in Genesis 1:26–27, which reveals God saying: "'Let us make man in our image, after our likeness; and let them have dominion over the fish of the sea, and over the birds of the air, and over the cattle, and over all the earth, and over every creeping thing that creeps upon the earth". So God created man in his own image, in the image of God he created him; male and female he created them'. He thereafter took the participants through other spiritual passages to drive home his message and concluded that 'salvation history is consummated in "the wedding Feast of the Lamb"' (Rv 19:7–9). He further stated that 'the primordial form in which humanity bears God's image and likeness is the marital covenant'.

Having been personally touched by the spiritual message of Dr Hahn, I found myself blessed again to listen to the all-inspiring spiritual presentation of Cardinal Luis Antonio Tagle of Manila, the Philippines. His highly acknowledged keynote address, which was recorded and made available to the participants the next day, needs to be played back regularly by families for the spiritual benefit of all the family as there is quite a lot to learn from it as to how to make our domestic church functional. His address inspired thousands of people to rise at different times to give him a standing ovation. Having earlier expected that his address would make a great impact on all of us, I decided to use my phone video camera to cover the entire address to play it back a number of times for my family members and members of the Holy Family Society who could not attend the World Meeting of Families in Philadelphia.

Cardinal Tagle certainly overwhelmed everyone with his knowledge and spiritual gifts, as he reminded all about the various wounds we suffer every day, pointing out that the pains of these wounds are meant to be joined with the suffering that Christ himself experienced while in the world. Some of these pains he enumerated as loneliness, poverty, disability, illness, drug addiction, unemployment, etc. He therefore reasoned that if we identify ourselves with Christ, we must walk with each other in love and support, beginning with our family members and those in our Churches. He made it clear that it is due to the love he personally has for his family that he himself came to Philadelphia with his own parents.

This impressed everyone because of the practical example he demonstrated. He emphasised that the Church is our mother and teacher as well as our comforter and guide. The cardinal pointed out that the Church is consequently our family who is blessed with many children, some of whom she placed on our way to attend to our spiritual and material needs, while some others with greater needs are to be attended to by ourselves.

Cardinal Tagle made everyone understand that the sufferings we encounter in this world, including the sufferings that come our way in our attempt to help others, 'cannot be compared with the glory that will be revealed and given to us' (Rm 8:18) when it pleases God to call us from this earth. He then raised two questions: How can we therefore help each other? And how can the Church bring the healing power of God's grace to members of her family?

In a way, he also provided answers to these questions. He effortlessly took us through practical ways of being our brother's keeper, bringing out scriptural passages to enrich our faith as well as taking time to provide answers to complex questions that were hitherto bothering us.

Listening to Cardinal Tagle's message on pain and suffering, one is immediately reminded of Pope Francis' call that we all need to get out of ourselves to identify with the poor; feel their pains, and suffer with them. He also wants the whole Church to show more concern for the poor and the sufferings of her members. Pope Francis prefers to see the Church in the forefront, waging war against poverty and sufferings in the land without her losing her primary focus.

Was there any wonder therefore when he stunned the entire world by his honest, down to earth message, as previously mentioned in Chapter Four, indicating very strongly in one of his remarks in *Evangelii Gaudium* (no. 49) that:

I prefer a Church which is bruised, hurting and dirty because it has been out on the streets, rather than a Church which is unhealthy from being confined and from clinging to its own security. I do not want a Church concerned with being at the centre and then ends by being caught up in a web of obsessions and procedures. If something should rightly disturb us and trouble our consciences, it is the fact that so many of our brothers and sisters are living without the strength, light and consolation born of friendship with Jesus Christ, without a community of faith to support them, without meaning and a goal in life. More than by fear of going astray, my hope is that we will be moved by the fear of remaining shut up within structures which give us a false sense of security, within rules which make us harsh judges, within habits which make us feel safe, while at our door people are starving and Jesus does not tire of saying to us: 'Give them something to eat' (Mk 6:37).

Meanwhile, some of the photographs taken of some of our Nigerian delegation who attended the events in Milan, will be published below. This will be in Appendix C, where we intend to show pictorially how pleasant it is to be at the World Meeting of Families. It is hoped that this will take the message of solidarity, friendship and common faith to the doorsteps of many Christians and non-Christians alike.

From the report given above and the one following in Chapter Five on the World Meeting of Families held in Dublin, Ireland, in August 2018, the reader will be able to see the usefulness of family members making themselves available to attend the triennial international event being organised by the Dicastery for the Laity, Family and Life at the Vatican.

On this note, the reader can move on to the report on Dublin in the next chapter where there is the opportunity for everyone to read the testimonies of one of my daughters and one of my granddaughters, who were both with me in Dublin along with some other members of my family entourage.

May Jesus, Mary and Joseph continue to use the World Meeting of Families to promote friendship and unite families of different nations, as well as provide protection for human lives in the world. And may the almighty God give us all the wisdom, intelligence, energy, freedom and the wherewithal we need to faithfully serve him and humanity in our chosen vocations.

Holy Family: Be our model and our inspiration!

6

Domestic Church:
Experiences From the
World Meeting of Families
in Dublin

The World Meeting of Families was held in Dublin, Ireland from 21–26 August 2018. It was guided by the theme, 'The Gospel of the Family: Joy for the World'. This major international event brought together families from across the world to celebrate, pray and reflect upon the central importance of marriage and the family as the builder and the sustainer of our domestic church, of our universal Church and of our society at large.

The gathering of families from different parts of the world in Dublin in 2018 had, at its heart, the following key moments:

(a) 21 August 2018, a National Opening of the World Meeting of Families (WMOF2018), which took place simultaneously in all the different dioceses of Ireland.

(b) 22–24 August 2018, a three-day Congress that gave a tremendous spiritual package to all the participants to take home. Each day, and each presenter of papers, reflected on different subjects but all directed towards increasing our knowledge on the general theme of the world meeting as chosen by the Holy Father, Pope Francis. In the package, there were also many spiritually enriching programmes for adults, youths and children, all held simultaneously in different locations within the venue. The Congress included the daily celebration of the Eucharist, prayerful activities, exhibitions, cultural events and musical performances.

(c) Saturday, 25 August 2018, Festival of Families, comprising a reflective concert style event within a prayerful and joyful atmosphere, in which personal stories of faith were shared by families from all the continents in the world.

(d) Sunday, 26 August 2018, WMOF 2018, Pope Francis presided over the solemn Eucharistic Celebration that was attended by seventy thousand people from Ireland and all over the world.

The theme song for the World Meeting of Families 2018 was 'The Joy of Love', which substantially echoed the joy of the family of Christ, a family that even when broken, bowed or wounded, has a hope that shines brightly in the darkness. There was a great joy among the people who came from all the continents of the world to learn, to interact and to celebrate.

Over the course of the week of the World Congress, there was an ambitious programme with an impressive lineup of speakers, who warmed our hearts with specific spiritual messages, followed by scintillating music and songs. We also had perpetual adoration. Like the other pilgrims, I spent three days racing to the Conference Halls, where I got much more than what I expected, leaving inspired and humbled, challenged and enriched. What more could we ask for?

As expected, there were numerous different subjects that centred on the unique dignity and value of every human being and the importance of the family as a school for learning Christian values. Around 80 per cent of the contributors were lay speakers, mostly couples, while around 20 per cent were clergy and religious.

On the first day, there was a presentation by Cardinal Luis Antonio Tagle that sparked *spiritual fire* at the arena. The title of his address was 'Choose Life: Pope Francis on the 'throwaway' Culture'.

In his appealingly good-humoured way, Cardinal Tagle traced the history of planned 'throwaway culture' and the production of goods with an artificially limited useful purpose and linked this to a culture of viewing people as expendable. Drawing on Pope Francis' two books *Laudato Si*, on the care for our common home, and *Amoris Laetitia*, the Joy of Love, he talked about how, in our present world, people can be viewed in a 'transactional fashion' and treated as commodities.

Referendum on Abortion

Referring to the recent referendum on abortion in Ireland, which gave legal status to abortion, Cardinal Tagle saw it as a confirmation of the 'throwaway' culture that Pope Francis hammered on in his books. He pointed out that the unborn child, the elderly, the sick and those with disabilities, prisoners, migrants and those who have been victims of human trafficking are often discarded, cast aside as being of lesser value.

In his homily, during the Mass in the Family Arena, Archbishop Eamon Martin, Archbishop of Armagh and Primate of all Ireland, spoke eloquently of the key place of the family in the society, quoting Pope St John Paul II who once indicated that: 'As the family goes, so goes the nation and so goes the whole world in which we live'.[1] He then emphasised that the welfare of the family is crucial to the welfare of the world, pointing out that supporting families in all their complexity should be a prime consideration of those concerned with promoting the common good of the society. He urged all to approach our politicians and ask them: To what extent do their policies support families and life?

The week of the congress was certainly of great grace. The various speakers on topics affecting families included Dr Mary Aiken on

[1] Pope John Paul II, Apostolic Pilgrimage to Bangladesh, Singapore, Fiji Islands, New Zealand, Australia and Seychelles *Homily of Pope John Paul II* on 30 November 1986, 4, Perth, Australia, 1986.

turning technology to the greater good, talks on marriage; marriage preparation and sexuality in marriage, and a harrowing account of human trafficking from Maya, a survivor of slavery and abuse. There were other topics that explored every possible family situation and every challenge that families face from time to time. Many participants who listened to these spiritual talks were amply satisfied with the spiritual benefits that came their way, which they were happy to take home to share with others who could not make it to the World Meeting.

Spiritually Inspired Talk

This was why Bishop Robert Barron of the Archdiocese of Los Angeles who gave another spiritually inspired lecture described the forum as 'the place par excellence for the growth in virtue'. He told his audience that growing in virtue makes us truly free. Seeing the large crowds queuing to get into the hall for his talk, I pondered on how some atheists could have in their wildest dreams portrayed the Catholic faith as a relic of the past. Everyone in that gathering including the atheists saw such comments as completely off the mark. In fact, it could be seen that such a remark has emboldened thousands of the participants to go out to the whole world to strongly defend the Catholic faith everywhere.

There was no doubt that Bishop Barron's upbeat and insightful words attracted even the greatest cynic towards everything that the faith of Christ offers us and our families. It was also an eye-opener to many who did not know the profundity of the Catholic faith. He spoke mainly in a language that parents could understand about training their children; the self-giving that is central to true love and the challenges of trying to raise a child in the faith.

I was really uplifted and energised at seeing how many initiatives and projects have been started by different people; many of such initiatives were people's response to the social justice doctrine of the Church that includes reaching out to the poor, the homeless and the vulnerable. Those who had been dragged down by unrelenting negativity about the Church's activities left the Family Arena with bags full of books and other information materials, medals, souvenirs, etc. to take home for their loved ones. The greatest spiritual gift the participants received before their departure was the rekindling of their hearts with a great hope and love for one another; refueling everyone spiritually and making everyone ready to take on the task of evangelising the world.

Singing Joyfully to the Lord

Seeing the mothers, fathers, teenagers and small children singing joyfully together during the final Mass of the week, I felt that I had made a good decision from an early age to remain a Catholic throughout my lifetime. There was no doubting the fact that Pope Francis, the Dicastery of the Laity, Family and Life, the organisers at the Vatican, the selected speakers and the participants themselves brought joy to the whole world; and this joy is worth sharing with all peoples of the world, no matter their colour, race or country of origin. To conclude this chapter, I requested one of my daughters and one of my grandchildren who were at the World Meeting of Families in Dublin to bare their hearts on what they themselves witnessed. I wish you happy reading.

How the World Meeting of Families Has Continued to Influence My Life!

Clemetina E. Osunde (Second daughter of the author)
The World Meeting of Families (WMOF) to which my dad invited me to accompany him, took place in Dublin, Ireland, between 21–26 August 2018. It was an uplifting, fun, spirit-filled, week-long celebration packed with panel discussions, dance and musical concerts, exhibitions, cultural display and drama. Each day ended with a Mass – geared to engage every member of the family, from young babies to grandparents. Facilities were provided for the

different categories of people the organisers were hosting for the international event.

The theme of the meeting was: 'The Gospel of the Family: Joy for the World'. This resonated with me in such a personal way as I had been rediscovering the joyous and awesome presence of God, continuously for a couple of months leading up to the programme. This was happening in a way that I had not previously experienced. It seemed to me all through as if I were in my own bubble; but at the same time, I was able to share God's joy and presence with others.

During the course of that meeting, I met, interacted with and observed different families from various backgrounds with varied dynamics – all experiencing the joy of fellowship together as one big family. Some were young couples with children; some were young couples without children; some, single mothers; some, single fathers with their children and some were groups of youths who came together as a family, while others were grandparents with their families. It was truly inspiring to see the willingness of people, no matter their status in life, their countries of origin, or the language they speak, to all joyfully open themselves to the deepening of their faith and to the universal call to holiness.

There were a series of talks by keynote speakers, concerts, workshop, presentations, etc., all mapped out to further educate and entertain pilgrims throughout the period of the scheduled World Meeting of Families. I was able to attend a few of the talks, which were spiritually uplifting, educational and engaging. One of such talks, presented by Bishop Robert Barron, spoke to my heart. In that talk he reflected on Chapters Seven, Eight and Nine of the Pope's book, *Amoris Laetitia*, which he emphasised to be about formation within the moral and spiritual life of a person as well as the spirituality of the family.

The main point that struck me was the Pope's view of taking a more virtuous approach in adapting a spirit-filled life, as opposed to looking at the bible and the Church's teachings as just a set of rules. He stated that there was the need for us to be willing to walk towards being, and doing good, on a continual basis. This becomes our moral compass, our everyday behaviour, which then creates virtue in us, in the way we deal with our families; with people around us, in our communities, in our environment and indeed in the world at large. He pointed out that the Pope sees the family as a key source of our formation, the first school of virtue.

He also went on to talk about the challenges the use of technology is placing on our families. He noted that we seem to be living in a world where we are instantly gratified, leaving little or no room for patience, which is the main source of virtue. This talk gave me a lot to reflect on, not just during my time in Dublin but also when I got back home. I thought about my upbringing, challenges I have faced growing up and still face to this day. I have come to appreciate that I am where I am today because of the grace of God. I thought of my relationship with my family, my son and people around me. I found the need to never give up on trying to do better. To be better and to be willing to burnout so that others can live to give glory to God.

I have come to understand what my purpose in life is. I use music and food to share God's love in this world. This explains why I am in my Church's choir and being fully involved in the Church's charitable programmes. I have been part and parcel of the Church's charitable works for more than fifteen years. It is my fervent desire to continue to let God use me as a vessel to do his will, and to also help me to fulfil the purpose for which he created me to be in this world.

Let me conclude this short piece by saying that the World Meeting of Families, which I had the opportunity to attend with my dad, my senior sister and her daughter, and Rev. Fr Richard Ademujimi, really impacted on my life and has made me to be more focused on the little things that I can do to make life more interesting for people around me. This is where I find my strength and my joy today, and I am quite pleased with myself and my family for preparing me for my new apostolate.

My Experience at the World Meeting of Families and How It Has Affected My Life

Glenda Oloke (Fifteen-year-old granddaughter of the author)

The World Meeting of Families, 2018 edition, was held in Dublin, Ireland, from 21–26 August. Many families across the globe gathered during this week to celebrate their faith, share experiences and testimonies, and above all to contemplate all the challenges thrown at us in life but most importantly to pray and worship our God as one big family. The theme of the congress was: 'The Gospel of the Family: Joy for the World'.

Day One: Arriving in Dublin was quite exciting and joyful for me as I had never been there before. It was very fascinating for me to see thousands of families from around the world with different dressing styles or habits. I travelled there with my mother, my aunt and my grandfather who requested me to write about my experience when we returned back to London. I remember that our family delegation from London was later joined by Rev. Fr Richard Ademujimi from Nigeria. My grandmother could not make it because she had earlier travelled to the USA for urgent family issues.

So, we were five in our delegation to Dublin, where we met a huge delegation from Nigeria. We all arrived in Dublin on the 21 August 2018 and began our registration for the event that same day but completed it in the morning hours of the next day, 22 August. There was an opening speech in the main conference arena after which we were presented with the order of events taking place in the different conference halls properly equipped for the World Meeting of Families. This made the participants from different nations follow the lectures using translating gadgets. We were quite thrilled to listen to the very welcoming message from Pope Francis with the aid of the translating earphones that were provided to each participant!

Being Obedient and Good to Our Parents

Days Two, Three and Four: This was a three-day congress filled with different speeches, performances and programmes for adults, youths and children. My experience in taking part in the youth programmes was fantastic and lively! Every day, we experienced many talks from priests and also other religious leaders. These talks stressed the importance of always being obedient and good to our parents and elders, particularly those who are senior to us in our family. Following my upbringing, this was not strange to me because I myself have been trying to implement this in my own life.

Every evening of the congress day, we enjoyed Gospel music concerts and performances from different highly acclaimed artists. The concerts were extremely spiritual and uplifting. Seeing other Catholic youths like myself, engaging and performing in these activities encouraged me to take a firm decision to be more active in Church activities. So, on my arrival back to London I joined my Church choir at the Holy Apostles Catholic Parish in Pimlico. This today makes me quite happy as I feel quite fulfilled after singing during the Mass each Sunday. I am also currently helping to coordinate the youth group in the parish.

Day Five: The Festival of Families was a very vibrant and colourful setting. Many people from around the world shared their personal testimonies and journeys in faith as a family. Just like the theme for the year, joy was definitely brought to every participant. Any time I have the chance to advise my fellow youths, I will always let them know that as young people, we must know that we have to meet certain standards in society as our parents expect us to be good models for other youths. In addition, we need to be proud of our Catholic faith as this naturally brings us joy, especially when we remain focused in life.

Spiritual Ambience Everywhere

Day Six: Pope Francis led a final celebration of the Holy Mass, which thousands of people attended. There was such a spiritual and prayerful ambience at this event that made me feel the urge to carry on praying more and spending more time, particularly on Sundays, in worshipping God.

On arriving back home from Dublin, I took to reading more of the *YouCat* book that I received as a gift in Dublin and spending more time saying prayers to God in times of need. I must use this opportunity to thank my grandfather who asked my mother and myself to join his delegation to Dublin. I also wish to thank God who showered his blessings on us and spared our lives throughout the pilgrimage. My prayer is also for all youths to live a more prayerful life and bring joy to themselves as they sincerely wish others peace of mind and body.

May the good Lord bless and prosper our faith as we reflect on the benefits of having the triennial World Meeting of Families, as a way of uniting families in the world. I hereby advise parents not to deny their children the opportunity of attending the World Meeting of Families since there are always very interesting and educative pogrammes for the youths who are also members of their individual families.

7

Domestic Church and the New Evangelisation Mission: Experiences of Christian Families

While preparing to write this book, I felt that it would be quite useful and beneficial for the reader to have a bird's eye view of the experiences of Christian families who have, for some time, shown a keen interest in making their domestic church functional and spiritually beneficial for people in their household. This was why I invited families across the board to write true-life stories about their experiences. It was made clear to them that it was the intention of the Holy Family Society to put on the shelf for everyone, Christians and non-Christians alike, new books on the domestic church as part of its efforts to impress on family members throughout the world the need to pay much more attention to the development of their family spirituality.

It is the belief of the Church and our own conviction that Christians and non-Christians can do more to develop their spirituality by returning, first and foremost, to their roots to make beneficial use of their homes by organising themselves into family praying groups with a view to living the lives exemplified by the early Apostles and the disciples of Christ. The Holy Family Society also believes that some families among us who already have a lot of experience in organising their prayer devotions in the comfort of their homes can help to direct others on what to do to achieve a peaceful and life-changing environment. Many of such families were therefore targeted to be reached in order to obtain their testimonies. Only a few of those that were reached turned in their testimonies, out of which three are published below.

It is also to be noted here that when family members come together daily in the home for family devotion, the domestic church sprinkles out a lot of spiritual gifts on the participants, making the home not only spiritually buoyant but also filled with happiness. This is one of the special benefits of praying together as a family.

We therefore see it as a good thing for many growing families to learn from the initiatives of keen followers of Christ, especially regarding the steps taken by them to keep their domestic churches functioning in the last ten or more years. The spiritual benefits received by members of participating families are what we are presenting in this chapter as a stimulus to help wake up many Christian and non-Christian families who are desirous of receiving more blessings from God. It is our belief that if those planning for their marriages and young couples study the experiences of others who have been ten or more years in marriage, they will certainly have something good to learn from their shared experiences.

Pope Francis on the New Evangelisation Mission

The reader may recall that our Holy Father, Pope Francis, has made it explicitly clear that those who want to be seriously engaged in the new evangelisation mission must be ready to tell their own stories that could form an 'appendix' to the holy bible. It is not a question of blowing one's trumpet but to be employed as a genuine attempt to use one's own story to open the door to evangelisation if we really embark on a crucial mission to evangelise others. This is anchored on the fact that what one does not have, one cannot give.

The Pope in his message on the Fifty-fourth World Communications Day on 24 May 2020, warned about the stories we accept for the purpose of evangelisation because 'not all stories are good stories', he emphasised. He went further to remind us of a bad story that is told of the serpent who deceived Eve to eat of the forbidden fruit in the Garden of Eden. He said that this serpent successfully deceived Eve by telling her: "'When you eat of it … you will be like God" (cf. Gn 3:4)'. The Pope then pointed out that:

> The temptation of the serpent introduces into the fabric of history a knot difficult to undo. 'If you possess, you will become, you will achieve …' This is the message whispered by those who even today use storytelling for purposes of exploitation. How many stories serve to lull us, convincing us that to be happy we continually need to gain, possess and consume. We may not even realise how greedy we have become for chatter and gossip, or how much violence and falsehood we are consuming. Often on communication platforms, instead of constructive stories which serve to strengthen social ties and the cultural fabric, we find destructive and provocative stories that wear down and break the fragile threads binding us together as a society. By patching together bits of unverified information, repeating banal and deceptively persuasive arguments, sending strident and hateful messages, we do not help to weave human history, but instead strip others of their dignity.[1]

In the same message, the Pope also directed us as to what story we should entertain for the purpose of evangelisation. He said, among other things, that what we need to take to the field for evangelisation purposes is the 'story that renews us'. According to the Pope, our own story should become a 'part of every great story'. He further stated that:

---

[1] Pope Francis, *Message of His Holiness Pope Francis for the 54th World Communications Day*, 2, Rome, 2020.

As we read the scriptures, the stories of the saints, and also those texts that have shed light on the human heart and its beauty, the Holy Spirit is free to write in our hearts, reviving our memory of what we are in God's eyes. When we remember the love that created and saved us, when we make love a part of our daily stories, when we weave the tapestry of our days with mercy, we are turning another page. We no longer remain tied to regrets and sadness, bound to an unhealthy memory that burdens our hearts; rather, by opening ourselves to others, we open ourselves to the same vision of the great storyteller. Telling God our story is never useless: even if the record of events remains the same, the meaning and perspective are always changing. To tell our story to the Lord is to enter into his gaze of compassionate love for us and for others. We can recount to him the stories we live, bringing to him the people and the situations that fill our lives. With him we can re-weave the fabric of life, darning its rips and tears. How much we, all of us, need to do exactly this![2]

Using True-Life Stories to Evangelise Others

The Pope's message gave us a good bearing on how to search for down-to-earth, true-life stories that can positively impact on people's lives, with a view to converting them and encouraging them to give up their old ways of life. It is only when such people return to the warm embrace of the Lord along with members of their families that we can really claim that our efforts are yielding a bountiful harvest. The type of stories we are encouraging people to arm themselves with when going into the field for evangelisation are published below. Happy reading.

First is the testimony of Mrs Ivonne Ruiz, whose family members worship at St Brendan's Catholic Church, Miami, Florida, USA:

---

[2] Pope Francis, *54th World Communications Day*, 5.

Benefits of Our Domestic Church
By Ivonne Ruiz

In my experience, the benefits of our domestic church have mainly been spiritual.

The beginning of our domestic church, our marriage, grew from our meeting within the community of the Church. It was easy to see that God himself brought us together; we met at our parish's Young Adult Group. Even before the sacrament of marriage, we attended Mass together and were blessed with our common Catholic faith. My husband had entered into a civil marriage when he was very young, and was divorced, with a little four-year old daughter when I met him. From the start of our domestic church we were already three people, with the responsibility of teaching the faith to a child who had experienced the divorce of her parents. It is always a challenge to teach a child who has been affected by divorce to still believe in the sanctity and indissolubility of marriage. By the grace of God, we provided for my stepdaughter what she has described in her own words as 'the best example of what a loving Christian marriage should be'. She in turn was able to believe in marriage and later chose a loving Christian man as her husband.

In addition, God has blessed us with six more wonderful children. The spiritual benefits of becoming parents have been innumerable. The sacrifice and utter denial of self that is required to be a parent, particularly of many children, and the love and support my husband and I have given to one another in order to fulfil this awesome responsibility, is clearly the grace of God who wishes our domestic church to mirror the love of the Holy Trinity. Other benefits are the patience and forgiveness necessary for eight unique people to daily live together within 1400 square feet. We have also experienced such immense gratitude for our health, for the blessing of having all of our needs met, for all of the joys we have experienced together, and also for the strength of the Holy Spirit when we have experienced the sorrowful times. I also feel that our domestic church is a rock of strength as we try to swim against the current of the secular culture in which we live. The truth, the answers to the most important questions in life, will be found here in our domestic church, because we are guided by the universal Church.

Our Lives Not About Us
Living in a large family also helps each of us to remember something very important: the world does not revolve around us. We are daily reminded in our domestic church of the truth that our lives are not about us, but rather about God's purpose for us. We begin to see first in the domestic church that we are here to serve one another. We learn to give and to receive love.

Another spiritual benefit of our domestic church is that we have gotten better at figuring out what matters most, and what matters least. We have been forced to learn the difference between needs and wants. I suppose this could translate into a material benefit of our domestic church: being good stewards of the material gifts that God has given us.

The second testimony is from a Nigerian family. It was sent in by Mrs Georgiana O. Ogbutor on behalf of her blessed family. Happy reading.

The Benefits of Our Domestic Church
By Mrs Georgiana Ogochukwu Ogbutor
I would like to describe our domestic church by using the parable of the mustard seed in Matthew 13:31–32. The mustard seed, which is the smallest of all seeds grows up to become a big tree where many birds come to make their nests. Our domestic church started in earnest when my children (four in number) were growing up. We used to wake up around 5 a.m. every day to pray our family rosary, along with some other prayers, and then recite Psalm 51 and chant Psalm 23 to conclude the prayers. Having continually received a lot of blessings and favours from the Lord through the intercession of our

Blessed Virgin Mary, we have been kept together in love and unity in our family. We also attend morning Mass most of the times together and occasionally pay visits to the Blessed Sacrament.

The Book of Proverbs 22:6 says: 'Train up a child in the way he should go, and when he is old, he will not depart from it'. The mustard seed that was planted on the day of our Catholic marriage continued to multiply as we were continuously blessed with children. Our family has been continuously nurtured by Jesus and his Mother Mary since we got married, hence we can afford to praise and worship him every day in the comfort of our homes, in the Church and in our places of work.

Already, our grown up children have gotten married, and now have their own children. They have happily extended their Christian life and morals to their own children. It is of great joy to us today to see our grandchildren following their own biological parents to attend morning Mass as they have seen it practised in the family. Our children have kept the tradition of family prayer going as a routine.

Persevering in Difficult Times

So, with joyful hearts, we are using this opportunity to thank the almighty God for the numerous spiritual benefits we have received in our domestic church, especially for giving us the strength and wisdom to persevere in difficult times, and for extending these special gifts to our extended family members. It is gratifying to note here that the new internet facilities are helping us to stick together in spite of being separated by distance as we organize Zoom prayer meetings from time to time. This enables those in the United States of America to participate in family prayers with us in Nigeria.

Every day in our home, we still wake up early in the morning to say the rosary with our wards before proceeding for morning Mass. We attribute all the family blessings and protection we have been enjoying in the family over the years to the intercession of the Queen of Heaven, the Blessed Virgin Mary, and to our Lord Jesus Christ.

It is pertinent to mention here that my biological mother of blessed memory contributed positively to my spiritual growth. All the prayers and songs I learnt from her, I also taught my children thereby keeping up the faith, and using every opportunity to sing praises to God.

In conclusion, the importance of the domestic church cannot be overemphasised in our Christian life, because the small mustard seed that was sown decades ago, has now grown to a giant tree with the help of God. Our plea here is for every Catholic family, in fact every Christian family, to have a functioning domestic church. Those who make good use of it will be amazed at the spiritual and material benefits they will certainly receive in God's own time.

My Life, the World Meeting of Families and Our Domestic Church

By Dr Mrs Marian Imaze Davis

I cannot fully express in words my enthusiasm in sharing my life's journey before and after attending the World Meeting of Families in Milan, Italy in 2012, and then in Philadelphia, in September 2015. Today is 2 July 2020, almost five years since my family journeyed from our home in Miami, Florida, and attended the World Meeting of Families that forever changed my life and the life of my family.

Firstly, in order to appreciate the testimony of my life, I would like to take you on a little journey. I hope in this journey I will enlighten you on who I am and where I came from and most importantly, demonstrate to you the spiritual restoration of my life and the life of my domestic church after my attendance of the WMOF. All that I can say here without mincing words is that my family reflects God's goodness and love.

As a form of introduction, the reader may want to know that I, Imaze Marian Davis, am the fifth child of Sir David and Dame Mary-Joan Osunde. My parents brought up their seven biological children, along with their numerous extended family of cousins, aunties and uncles in a loving, strong Catholic home. One would think that

Catholicism runs for generations in our family, but in actuality, our roots in Catholicism sprout from my father's curiosity when he was a young boy. I will allow him to share his story in his autobiography.

I, on the other hand, was born and raised a Catholic. I was born in the ancient city of Benin, in Nigeria. As a child, I always knew I had a special relationship with Jesus. The memory of our home in Benin centres on the image of our family's altar table and a wall with a picture of the Sacred Heart of Jesus and a large white beaded rosary hanging over it. This rosary would glow in the dark, many nights when we were faced with no light due to power outage. I was like any other child afraid of the dark and hoped to be somewhere close to the front door during a power outage where I could seek comfort from the moonlight or the neighbour's gas light beaming through the doors and quickly reunite with other family members and friends sitting outside and sharing stories and jokes.

The Presence of the Holy Trinity in the Home

Often, the glowing rosary in the dark was not only the light that led me to the front door of the house but it was a reminder that I was not alone in the dark as the Mother of our Lord, Jesus Christ, our crucified Christ himself and his Father in heaven, as well as the Holy Spirit, were all present with us in the home. One particularly important thing that I remember as a little child was watching my parents practise our Catholic faith in action. I watched them turn small events to lifelong traditions that became imbedded in our Catholic family and community.

Firstly, it was one Christmas night when we were visited by the local Church choir of St Maria Goretti for the Annual Festival of Carols. After that joyful musical event, my father began the annual Christmas Carol Night Singing Competitions among local Catholic choirs in the parishes in Benin City, and later extended this to the whole archdiocesan choirs. Another event was visiting the prisons the day before Christmas and feeding the prisoners and sharing gifts.

This was an eye opener for myself and my siblings as we realised how fortunate we were to have our freedom, and to live with our parents sheltering us and teaching us good morals and how to live out our faith. It was this yearly visit to the prison yard that made us all realise how people can lose their freedom and be denied the opportunity of living with their loved ones.

Dining With Persons With Disabilities

Every Sunday after Mass, my parents would, as a matter of routine, take us to St Joseph's House, a shelter home for persons with disabilities. We shared and ate lunch with them and spent some quality time laughing, singing and praying. Fr Bill Scanlon, SJ, who now resides outside New York in the USA, was then the Parish Priest of St Joseph's Catholic Church, Benin City.

Soon, my parents transcended all these Sunday experiences to an everlasting experience of giving, sharing and caring, especially for the most vulnerable among our society. The Sir David Osunde Foundation for persons with disabilities was born. I watched my father challenge the Church, tribal leaders and even the local government in Benin City, Nigeria, to acknowledge persons with disabilities and to stop the stereotype that their disability was some kind of punishment from God or a misfortune from bad deeds.

Some elders in our society back then and still today believed heavily in paganism. They believed that disabilities whether congenital or acquired were a kind of curse or misfortune inflicted by oneself. Persons with disabilities would attend Mass outside the Church or would be trampled on while entering the Church with little recognition. Most of them were beggars at the Church's gate asking for small amounts of money to feed their families.

Every year, I watched my parent's determination for change in this aspect of people's lives yielding fruitful returns as Church pews were redesigned to have persons with disabilities sitting comfortably at the front pews or in their wheelchairs in the front of the Church.

This simple milestone sent a huge welcoming message to those who had been forgotten and isolated for centuries. For once, the rich and the famous who filled the front pews in Church were then faced with a choice to be in the front pews with persons with disabilities or to look elsewhere to find other seats. Everyone was thereby reminded in the Church without any spoken word about the equality of all children of God, regardless of disabilities. With that little act, many in the Church and in our community were encouraged to embrace this work of charity as a formidable project that can bring a lot of relief to the less privileged in society.

Home for Persons With Disabilities

As my father's foundation grew in magnitude in terms of the enrolled persons with disabilities, so was the exponential growth in awareness of our nation, Nigeria, and its leaders. My mother, Mary-Joan Osunde went on to realise her dream of a home for persons with disabilities. In that home, she provided accommodation for young children whose parents were struggling to care for them. As a child who watched carefully my parents' missionary works, I often asked God what my calling would be.

What I found then was that my life journey took me to a Catholic school in England at the age of nine. As I settled down in the new school, I never once felt my Catholic faith and teaching was challenged. The memory of the life-changing experience of home in Nigeria had set for me a solid foundation that had cemented my love for my Catholic faith and my innermost relationship with God.

At age 16, I would set out again on another journey to study medicine in the United States but this time away from all my siblings. Looking back now, I believe I had reached a part of life's journey that only I was to journey. In this journey of faith, I would come to meet strangers who would become pillars to building my domestic church. I was fortunate to have a guardian, Dr Titilayo Ufomata, who was a professor at Kentucky State University and a devoted Catholic.

The Good Shephard Catholic Church in Franklin County, Kentucky, became my new parish and I was blessed and fortunate to have Dr Ufomata pick me up every Sunday from my university campus to attend Mass at the local parish. After Mass, we would sit and enjoy each other's company, sharing a warm Sunday meal and reflect on the joy of family and friendship.

Another stranger that was divinely placed in my life to begin my domestic church was my college classmate and best friend Tyree Davis who grew up attending the International Church of Christ, a non-denominational church. My domestic church really began when I had to answer God's calling to stay with my Catholic faith, attending weekly Mass even though I was in college miles away from home.

My Meeting With a Future Partner in the University

That commitment to myself was not enough as God had great plans for me to enjoy that calling and blessings with a life partner and create great offspring to work in God's vineyard. I honestly believe God sent me my husband, Tyree Davis, as an angel who would not only know my innermost heart but be a spiritual companion ready to walk with me on this journey of faith.

The life's journey of faith that we began on 20 November 1999, in Frankfort, Kentucky State, initiated the foundation for our domestic church when we began to attend the Good Shepherd's Catholic Church together every Sunday.

Four years later, I returned home to London with Tyree where we formally sealed the foundation of our domestic church with our marital vows at the Holy Apostles Catholic Church, Westminster, Pimlico, London, on 16 August 2003. Within ten years, God endowed our young family with five children.

As I reflect now on the ten years of our lives between the year that we got married and the year we attended the World Meeting of Families in Milan, Italy in 2012, and then consecutively the one held in Philadelphia, Pennsylvania in September 2015, I can only look back with gratitude knowing the tremendous blessings on our marital and spiritual lives.

Balancing Work With Family Life

Like most couples and many Catholic families, my husband and I struggled with the challenge of balancing work and family. I, a podiatric physician, had dedicated the majority of my time to patient care and wellbeing. It has been my own resolve to practice medicine with the highest devotion to my work and calling, without giving chance to frivolities. Often at some very tough times, I find myself questioning my calling to medicine because of the inability to balance work with my prayer life, along with my spouse and kids.

In 2012, my parents, Sir David and Dame Mary-Joan Osunde, had received a special invitation from the Vatican, as members of the Pontifical Council for the Family, to attend the World Meeting of Families in Milan. As special arrangements were made for them, my parents invited all members of our biological families as their special guests. After a conversation over the phone about booking their flights and hotel accommodation for their trip from Nigeria to Milan, my parents then informed us about other arrangements already being made for us to join the Nigerian group of delegates and members of the Holy Family Society who were scheduled to be in Milan.

We insisted that my husband and I were not prepared for an international trip as we had not planned for the children; apart from the fact that there was no arrangement in place for a fellow physician to have coverage for me during my absence from my private clinic. I also said that my husband had not also requested for work leave from his office as Federal staff. In spite of this initial state of unpreparedness, we found that to our amazement that things worked out for us within few days after the discussion. We found ourselves on a flight to Milan, Italy, on the day our parents were also scheduled to arrive there.

Developing Our Family Spirituality

Understanding that it was God's desire for us to experience what we called our first pilgrimage as a couple, we both attended the World Meeting of Families in Milan in a childlike manner, with an open mind and praying to God to teach us what family spirituality is all about. We specially asked for this because we heard our parents speaking about it from time to time. We also asked the almighty God to renew our Christian marital commitment to each other and to help make our domestic church more effective. It was a great opportunity to also pray fervently for our children.

Looking around the huge venue on our arrival at the Conference Centre, I was touched by the scene of so many large families with children of a similar age to our kids travelling from all parts of the world eager to attend the international event. Their demonstration of solidarity to their family, Catholic religion and to their country was overwhelming and captivating to my eyes. For the first time in my life, I saw an army of volunteer youths that came from different parts of the continents, spoke different languages, and assembled together for a common purpose of praising and worshipping God as well as serving him and humanity.

As I got myself engaged in multiple conversations with some of the youths, I understood how passionate they were about their Catholic faith and how they had heard God's calling to serve others. Their response to their calling was truly inspirational to me. I began to reflect on my own calling and to see the possibility of our children receiving a similar calling in their lives.

Leaving Our Worries at the Feet of Jesus

In summary, while in Milan, I found myself most *fired* by the teachings about *La Familia*. I had never thought so deeply about the sacredness of the family instituted by Christ until I attended the World Meeting of Families. I learnt that a significant effort must be put into the task of ensuring the spiritual growth of the family of

God. The emphasis of praying together and presenting all our life's worries and anxieties at the feet of Christ was most comforting to me.

Understanding that the devil is constantly wanting to destroy the family of God, which is our domestic church, we were informed about the need to be constantly alert to frustrate the work of the evil one. To do so, we were told to always arm ourselves with our rosary, saying it frequently whenever we have the opportunity in the home, in our office or during travelling time. We also learnt about patience and endurance and how to seek and show love in all that we do in life. It was emphasised that our holy desire for the love of God will naturally increase our own love for each other as husband and wife and for our children.

After the conference in Milan, we returned home to Miami, with both my husband and I feeling quite fulfilled in undertaking the trip. It gave us an opportunity, as it were, to renew our marriage commitment to each other.

It should not surprise anyone therefore that in 2015, my husband and I still had the burning desire to experience once again another World Meeting of Families. This time we made preparations to be in Philadelphia in the USA, for the Eighth World Meeting of Families.

Following our previous experience in Milan, with the children in their happiest mood, we decided to go to Philadelphia with the whole family. Without hesitation, we took the kids out of school and disrupted their academic learning, knowing fully and believing that the spiritual growth of their faith and of our domestic church was irreplaceable.

I watched our five children gaze at the crowd of attendees with awe and I felt as though the door of heaven had opened in their lives with God wanting to reveal himself to his little children.

Lifelong Opportunity and Experiences at the WMOF
The experience of attending the World Meeting of Families in Philadelphia with my parents, sibling, cousins, nieces, nephews as

well as my spouse and children, making twelve family members in all, was a lifelong opportunity that would forever be cherished. Most of the worries that weighed heavily on my mind about balancing my life with work and family are no longer a burden as they were then in 2012.

Today, with love in my heart, I am happy to testify with assertiveness the goodness of God in my life and in the life of my domestic church. God has endowed my husband and I with six loving and beautiful children and I can end by reflecting back on the truthfulness of Pope Francis' words in 2015 at the Festival of Families, when he said:

> God likes to give his love to open hearts. Do you know what he loves most? To knock on the door of families, and find families who love each other, who bring up their children to grow, and help them move forward. To create and develop a society with truth, goodness and beauty …
>
> Forgive me, but I have to say, the family is like a factory of hope. It's a factory of resurrection. God opened this path, this possibility …
>
> In the family, indeed, there are difficulties. But those difficulties are overcome with love. Hatred is not capable of dealing with any difficulty and overcoming any difficulty. Division of hearts cannot overcome any difficulty. Only love. Only love is able to overcome. Love is about celebration, love is joy, love is moving forward.[3]

I am not in doubt that a number of readers will find a lot to learn from the testimonies of people who have freely enrolled themselves here in the new evangelisation mission that the Holy Father, Pope

---

[3] Daniel Craig, *Philly Voice*, 'Transcript of Pope Francis' Improvised Festival of Families Speech', 27 September 2015, https://www.phillyvoice.com/transcript-pope-francis-festival-families-speech/; accessed on 2 July 2020.

Francis, has entrusted to each and every one of us. As indicated earlier, he has challenged us to tell our good stories and have them ready to accompany us as an 'appendix' to the holy bible as we go into the field for evangelisation purposes. His message at the Fifty-fourth World Communication Day is what one should reflect on regularly as we embark on the new evangelisation mission.

The Holy Family Society values this message very highly and has fully accepted it as a spiritual tool for evangelisation. This is because we believe that it is not enough to preach the Good News with great eloquence and forcefulness without valuable records of good works to back up the talks. The evangelisers in this new mission are to let their actions speak louder than their words.

Meanwhile, we are praying that enlightened Christian families reading the above will happily devote quality time to prepare their own testimonies, which could form part of the legacies they will happily leave behind for future generations. There is no denying the fact that family evangelisation is going nuclear because of the recent coronavirus pandemic. Everyone has to be ready to make effective use of one's domestic church, with a view to developing one's family spirituality. This is what families should crave for in order to constantly build on their relationship with God. A stitch in time saves nine, as our journey on earth must be directed towards eternal life.

So, if you want to be part of this spiritual programme, please endeavour to join the bandwagon of the Holy Family Society, which is championing the new evangelisation programme, with a view to helping families set up functioning domestic churches for the purpose of creating a conducive praying environment for members of the family to always be in the presence of God.

8

Domestic Church and God's Injunction: Be Fruitful, Multiply and Fill the Earth

From the scriptures and from what we see every day in the world, it is indisputable that one of the special gifts that God has given to humanity is pregnancy. This pregnancy has to be jealously guarded for nine months or thereabout before a child is born. The pains a woman in labour goes through before a child is born is indescribable but the joy that comes to the same woman minutes after childbirth is overwhelming and covers all the pains she had gone through in a minute. Her joy of having a newborn baby spreads to all members of her family, friends and well-wishers.

It is to be noted here that when God presents a family with a gift of pregnancy, it immediately becomes the responsibility of the married couples to care for the baby in the womb before it is born. How to care for the baby in the womb is an important subject that should be taught in the domestic church. This explains why I am quickly pointing this out before the reader gets to know more about the main subject of reflection in this chapter. Is there any wonder that I had written a separate book over twelve years ago on *Pregnancy, Naming Ceremony and Family Spirituality?* His Eminence, John Cardinal Onaiyekan, the former Archbishop of Abuja (now Emeritus) gave his blessing for the book to be read by Christians as he understandably and willingly provided the Imprimatur.

For everyone to understand why pregnancy is not only a special gift that no money in this world can buy, but also what God himself has designed to use as a special project to fulfil his injunction to humanity: 'Be fruitful, multiply and fill the earth' (Gn 9:1), there is the desired need to also discuss issues relating to this in the domestic church. The reason for this is to let everyone in the household understand the special role each and every one of them, including children, is to play to ensure that the baby in the womb is delivered safely on God's own date and time.

So, every pregnancy needs to be specially cared for, especially in a Catholic home where the couple know that there is no room for abortion, as such a thing is very much against Catholic teachings. It is to understand why God gave this special gift of pregnancy to humanity and how to care for it to fulfil God's purpose that I wrote the earlier book titled *Pregnancy, Naming Ceremony and Family Spirituality*. This book is available to be used in the domestic church to teach members of one's household the importance of pregnancy in the family and how to prayerfully care for the baby in the womb from month to month until the mother's delivery.

The book is also meant to help families prepare for the naming ceremony of the newly born baby and how to give him or her a heavenly-inspired name that will make him or her prosper in the Lord. The naming of a child is therefore an important spiritual exercise for the formal introduction of a new baby in the family to the community. This needs to be learned in the domestic church.

Since the book is already available, there will be no need to delve into detail here about what to do when there is a pregnancy in the family and how to use it to improve one's family spirituality. The main concern here is to bring God's injunction to the front burners of our hearts to remind everyone that as part and parcel of humanity, married couples are expected to 'Be fruitful, multiply and fill the earth'. This therefore becomes an important subject for adults and growing children to constantly reflect on in the domestic church.

Every Catholic who is married understands that a properly conducted marriage in the Catholic Church is indissoluble and that the married couple is therefore required to sustain this until God calls any of the spouses or both of them at the same time to glory and eternal rest as has happened in some cases in the past.

As millions of people who lived thousands of generations before us rightly understood, and as millions of those living in the present world today also understand, marriage is an institution that is ordained by God, and he, himself, guides it jealously to enable it to achieve its goal of making married couples co-creators with him so that, in his own time, human beings will undoubtedly fill the earth. This, to our mind, is why we have the biblical reference, indicating God's instruction to Noah and his sons, and by implication, to all of us, when he said: 'Be fruitful, multiply and fill the earth'. There is no indication anywhere in the bible that this noble directive was or is meant to be achieved in one generation. However, God directed that the future generations of Noah and his sons, i.e. the descendants after Noah and his sons, are meant to fulfil this task.

That is why from generation to generation, there has been a continuous increase in the world's population as married and unmarried people give birth to new life in their bid to answer God's call to 'Be fruitful, multiply and fill the earth'. This will continue until God's purpose for the marriage institution is achieved in the world.

God's Purpose for Creating Human Beings Must Be Fulfilled

So, no matter what the anti-life promoters do, and what those who are producing nuclear weapons and other chemical weapons of mass destruction do, God's purpose for the marriage institution will be fulfilled here on earth. And if God wants the whole world to be filled with human beings in one generation, or in one day, he could also do this because 'nothing is impossible to God' (Lk 1:37), and 'a thousand years are to Him, like a day that has passed' (Ps 90:4). No one should therefore be surprised if he decides to raise all those who have died thousands of years ago, in a second, to fill the whole universe if he wants to do this to fulfil his purpose. We therefore have no need to worry about the matter of when this world is to come to an end. This should be made clear to every participant in the activities of the domestic church.

All we need to emphasise here is that God expects us all to play our own part well in this world and leave the rest to him. We also need to place our trust in him and firmly believe that his purpose of creating the human being will be fulfilled on earth. Our belief should stem from what God himself manifests daily and mysteriously to our own knowledge. He makes the rain fall when he wills; he makes the sun shine when he wills; he makes the moon shine when he wills; he makes the earthquake occur when he wills and he makes the tsunami occur when he wills. Would anything then stop him from filling the earth with human beings at the time he wants?

The answer is no. Therefore, what he wants from married couples is to co-create with him and make the world a better place for everyone to live in. The yearly increase in the world's population alone is sufficient to confirm to us God's holy plan to have the world filled by human beings in his own time. Anyone doubting this may need to read from Isaiah 55:10–11 where God said: 'For as the rain and the snow come down from heaven and do not return there but water the earth, making it bring forth and sprout giving seed to the sower and bread to the eater, so shall my word be that goes forth from my mouth; it shall not return to me empty, but it shall accomplish that which I intend, and prosper in the thing I sent it'.

This undoubtedly confirms that God's purpose for creating human beings must be fulfilled. And there can be no question of there being too many human beings on this earth. From generation to generation, God has always provided for all human beings, even much more than he provides for the birds of the air. What has always happened from time immemorial is that there have been always greedy ones who deny others their rights and entitlements. This explains why there has always been poverty in the land from generation to generation among human beings.

Daily Happenings

In spite of the fact that the good things and wealth in the world are not evenly spread to all persons in the communities, God's love for everyone is the same. There is no discrimination in the amount of love God has for each person. He gives everyone the opportunity also to act like him by spreading the same genuine love while being one another's keeper. He designed this for the world to experience brotherliness, agape love, unity, justice and peace. To show us that this is what he designed for the world, he allows us to experience among other things, hot weather, cold weather, temperate climate, fertile land, the rainforest, sahara region, etc., without paying for any of them. In addition, we sleep and dream and wake at any time we want without paying for the duration of the sleep and the dreams we had as well as for our waking up at the time we desire.

But what we find in our dealing with each other in the world, is that those among us whom God has granted wisdom to discover anything, be it how to make a blade, toothbrush, cornflakes, soup ingredients, malaria drugs, coronavirus vaccines, chemical weapons, etc., sky-rocket their profits to such heights that the poor man or woman, the poor institutions and the poor nations of the world, will become poorer and poorer while their own wealth will continue to increase from day to day. This is the tragedy that the world is facing today and it must be addressed from the domestic church.

What we also need to bring to the understanding of every participant in the domestic church is that God in his kindness allows us to freely experience miracles in our own individual lives every day. What should immediately come to our minds are the miracles of our sleeping for many hours and waking up thereafter, in our eating food and building up our body parts from the day we were born, growing taller and/or older without knowing how and when it happens, our hair gradually turning from black to grey without knowing how and when it happens, in our shrinking as we get older after a certain point in life, etc. From these complex miracles, we will discover that our God is awesome and has the power to do anything with the human being he created in his image and likeness (Gn 1:26). Do we in fact, not also find anything mysterious in the human being bearing the image and likeness of God from one generation to another?

Our faith should make us believe that God can do what the human being thinks is impossible. In matters like this, faith is what we require to enable us to proceed in doing things that will lead us to God, knowing fully well that whatever we ourselves are capable of doing 'depends on faith' (Rm 4:16). All that we should bear in mind and teach in the domestic church is that God's promise to our forefather in faith, Abraham and his descendants, 'that they should inherit the world did not come through the law but through the righteousness of faith' (Rm 4:13).

It is for us not to doubt what God can do, especially in giving life to the dead, as the scriptures also inform us in Romans 4:17. Abraham, a man of great faith, believed that God 'gives life to the dead, and calls into existence the things that do not exist'. This explains why we need to believe that human beings will, in generations to come, fill the whole universe as desired by God. We should note that he who created the universe and who has ordered the future generations to come after Noah and his sons to 'be fruitful', will also ensure that humanity multiplies at a rate that will fill the earth.

Having known this, should we then continue to worry about the so-called population explosion being orchestrated by the Western world? Should we not be concerned more about how to get the greedy, wealthy nations, wealthy multinationals and the greedy, wealthy individuals in various nations to release their knees from the necks of weak and poor nations of the world so that they can *breathe* and experience the free air given to us by God?

With regard to the bringing of new life into this world, what all families should be concerned with is whether we have been obeying

God's injunctions on how a man and a woman should come together to become husband and wife. The questions that should agitate our minds at this point are:

(1) Are marriages being properly conducted as envisaged by God and in accordance with the teachings of the Catholic Church?

(2) Are pregnancies being seen as gifts of God to the family or are they being occasionally rejected and/or aborted by people in our family, in our community, in our society?

(3) What then should we do not to offend God's injunction: 'Be fruitful, multiply and fill the earth'?

These questions and many more should be our concern in our domestic church. Organising private workshops and/or seminars in the Church and/or in a family setting at home with experts on various topics to speak on these issues can be a good way of disseminating and sharing useful information to all participants in the activities taking place in the domestic church. With such an undertaking, God's message will be brought to the knowledge of many in our households. This will help many to understand and adopt the Christian ethics relating to marriage, pregnancy, natural methods that are available to families regarding the spacing of children, the spiritual care to be given to pregnancies and why the Church condemns abortion.

There is no doubt that millions of people before us busied themselves about what they could achieve with their marriages, regarding God's injunction, imploring us to 'be fruitful, multiply and fill the earth'. As earlier indicated, our own concern should be how to do our own part and leave the rest to God. We shouldn't worry much about whether we will be alive to see the time when human beings will fill the earth as God had ordered.

Our Role in Fulfilling God's Purpose for Creating Human Beings

Suffice it to know that every man or woman on earth is required to help fulfil God's purpose for the marriage institution. This could be done in many ways, five of which are:

(i) bearing children and adding to the population in the world.

(ii) promoting life, knowing that life is sacred and needs to be protected from the time of conception until God calls us home.

(iii) giving one's life completely to God in order to be in a position to give spiritual support to those entering into marital life as well as help to direct the living back to him.

(iv) supporting the poor, the weak, the elderly and the most vulnerable in the society to ensure that they do not leave this world before their time as a result of abandonment or inadequate care for human life.

(v) protecting the environment to ensure that the world around us is conducive for human beings to dwell in.

From what we have learnt from the scriptures and from our forefathers, coupled with the historical evidence available in the world, no human being, apart from our Lord Jesus Christ, who was both human and God, has been brought to life by being formed by the Holy Spirit in the womb of his or her mother. Our Mother Mary, the Immaculate Virgin, was blessed to have been the channel through which our Lord Jesus came to be born into the world, hence her title, the 'Blessed Virgin Mary'.

It is quite instructive to note here that since the birth of our Lord Jesus Christ over two thousand years ago, no other human being, living or dead, has been born like Jesus or known to have dropped from heaven to live in this world.

Since human beings are created 'in the image and likeness of God' every person living on this planet's life must be treated as sacred.

Therefore, we need to re-emphasise in the domestic church that no one has any right to terminate the life of any human being, from the time of conception to when God calls such a person back home to the great beyond. So, anyone who willingly destroys human life or contributes to the destruction of it while it is still maturing in the mother's womb or in the incubator, in the case of those born prematurely, can be said to be anti-life. Such a person is seen to be totally against God's injunction on marriage and human life.

It is needless to state here what awaits those who consciously destroy human beings formed in the image and likeness of God in the womb, or in the incubator where they are being cared for. This is because they have the option of reconciling themselves with our all-loving God. For us Christians, especially Catholics, it is most honourable, dignifying and God-fearing for us to be in the vanguard of promoting human life and the marriage institution. We have no excuse to do otherwise, especially as we know what God's injunction is with regard to marriage, that: 'a man leaves his father and his mother and clings to his wife, and they become one flesh' (Gn 2:24).

This is God's design for marriage. Any other form of marriage, be it what they term 'gay marriage', marriage between two women, marriage between a man and his pet dog, or such like, must be condemned in totality because they are not the types of marriages designed by God. They fall quite short of God's plan, as such marriages cannot be said to be in line with God's injunction: 'Be fruitful, multiply and fill the earth'. Those who have married according to God's plan are the ones who are expected to go forth after consummating their marriage to contribute their quota for the task of filling the earth, as they procreate with a great sense of responsibility.

Different Understanding of God's Plan for Marriage

It should be noted here that different denominations have their own understanding of God's command, instructing married couples to 'be fruitful, multiply and fill the earth'. This is why it should not surprise anyone when we find a Muslim, for instance, marrying four wives, with some of them still maintaining concubines with children born for them outside their own homes. Some traditionalists even marry more than four wives and have tens of children with many women outside their marital home. Maybe this is designed by themselves, or what is accepted by their own religion or cult as a way to quickly fill the earth.

Whether this is the case or not, the Christian should feel proud of his or her own understanding of the bible, while the Muslim should also feel proud of his or her own understanding of the Quran. Both are regarded by their adherents as holy books that should guide them throughout their lives.

As this author is only concerned with Christian marriage here, particularly Catholic sacramental marriage, there is the need to further ask a salient question to agitate our minds: What should a married Catholic do to sustain his or her marriage in order to model it after the Holy Family of Nazareth?

One thing to understand clearly from the start is that God did not make any mistake by giving Jesus, Mary and Joseph, the Holy Family of Nazareth, as a model for family life in the world.

The Need to Stick to God's Plan for Marriage

All Christians are therefore required to stick to God's plan for the marriage institution, with a view to promoting human life, which he graciously grants to us as the fruit of marriage. It is the way we do this that really shows the difference between Catholic marriages and other marriages in other denominations or in the Pentecostal churches around our street corners.

9

The Friends We Need to Help Develop Our Domestic Church

From the previous reports in Chapters Five, Six and Seven in this Volume Two and as indicated in Chapter Eight of Volume One, regarding the participation of family members in the World Meeting of Families, the reader will understand that being present in such a gathering provides ample opportunities for the participants to make international friends from different parts of the world. The fact that one is able to have direct, personal contact with hundreds of people and exchange greetings, contact addresses, emails and telephone numbers with a good number of them, helps greatly to unite the world, which is one of the objectives of hosting the triennial world meeting.

It is at such a gathering that one can really appreciate the marvellous work of God in creating human beings and distributing us to the different parts of the continents, making everyone in their different areas very unique. This is a point that was clearly made in Volume One of this book. It is being re-emphasised here to show the uniqueness of the human being, and why this unique gift of God in making each and every one of us in his image and likeness is to be used to activate our true love for him, which should be above all others, while at the same time creating genuine friendships with other human beings in the world.

As clearly indicated in Volume One, no one should be in doubt now that there are other numerous gifts of God to us as individuals. One of these gifts is freedom – the freedom to search within our own being for other special gifts, know them, appreciate them, and make good and profitable use of them all. It is when we do this, that we should expect to receive more gifts from him.

Our appreciation of what we have as special gifts from God and finding time to thank him for what he has given us on a platter of gold, also matters a lot.

Our Lord, Jesus Christ assures us that: 'to everyone who has, more will be given; but from him who has not, even what he has will be taken away' (Lk 19:26). This should encourage us to always make the best use of the special gifts we receive daily from God, most especially the gift of life. There is no doubting the fact that we hear of reports of those who went to bed but did not wake up. There are also daily reports of those who die in hospitals. And every day there are reports of those who died as a result of accidents on the roads or in plane crashes. Do we therefore not consider that it is by God's amazing grace and his loving kindness that, in spite of our unworthiness, we are still alive?

As our God has given every human being he created the very unique gift of his image and likeness, it behoves the people of the world to make good use of this special gift. Our ability to deal with fellow human beings whether in our local community or on an international level, with a view to bringing us all nearer to our God, becomes our own individual credit. This is why it is important for us to know that if we have the unique opportunity of attending any conference where God is placed at the centre of activities, we should use it profitably to make good friends, especially those that can help us to develop our relationship with our God.

It must be emphasised here that this is one of the lessons we should teach always in our domestic church. Be quite sure that if our children know this from the home, they will then understand the need to carefully choose their friends even in school. And if they do this, we should not only pride ourselves about the effective use of our domestic church, we should also count ourselves abundantly blessed by God.

It is also important for us to know that certain Christian principles or activities we learn from our friends can help us to develop our domestic church.

Therefore, exchanging ideas with friends one meets at conferences, either in a local or international setting, can help a great deal in advancing our family spirituality. In order for us not to forget our chance meetings with new Christian and non-Christian friends, it is very important that we should document these meetings with photographs, and then exchange addresses and phone numbers to enable us to continue building on the new friendship that God has placed on our path.

In international events such as the World Meeting of Families, one is always amazed to see how people from other continents rush to take photographs together, either because of one's national dress, the Christian love of sharing good things with one another, or the need to cultivate new Christian friendship, with a view to making the world a better place for all of us to live in.

Having now understood the need to build good relationships with others as we strive towards making the world a better place, while we daily work on improving our relationships with our God, our Creator, I wish to display in Appendix C some personal/family pictures of those who contributed the true-life stories in Chapters Six and Seven of this volume. There are also pictures of local and international events which some members of the Holy Family Society attended to expand their circle of friendship as well as carry on with their work of evangelisation.

Of particular note is the expansion of the members' circles of friendship in the Cameroon Republic and in the USA, where they went on evangelisation missions, and attended the World Meeting of Families, which took place in Philadelphia, USA, in 2015.

While urging the reader to spend some time in prayer for the people you see in the pictures in Appendix C, please note that we need to maintain genuine friendships with people, regardless of their colour, race, language, status in life, forms of disabilities, etc., to make our own lives easy-going, fruitful and focused on winning eternal life, together with our loved ones. This should be our goal.

It is hoped that, after taking a second look at these pictures, the reader will want to plan with his or her own family to become registered members of the Holy Family Society and move onwards to become active participants at the World Meeting of Families. The World Meeting of Families is usually organised every three years by the Vatican.

NOTE: For the benefit of those who want to participate in the future activities of the Holy Family Society which greatly help people to prepare for the World Meeting of Families as well as bring about the development of their domestic church, it is advisable that you contact the National Secretarial through her email: hfsnationalsecretariat@yahoo.com.

10

A Review of Volumes One and Two and a Preview of Volume Three

Having taken the reader through certain Christian principles we need to imbibe, and some crucial lessons we need to learn and put into practice before going on to family evangelisation, there is a need to look back and reflect on the topics covered in Volume One, and then in this Volume Two, to refresh the reader's memory. Thereafter, we can then have a preview of the topics to be dealt with in Volume Three of this book on the domestic church. This is being done in the hope that the reader has already spent quality time in going through Volume One before reading this Volume Two.

It is also hoped that the reader has found the reflections in Volume One and in this particular volume to be quite instructive, exciting, engaging and helpful in developing his or her domestic church. I expect that whatever the reader finds captivating, insightful and faith-building in what he or she has read so far, will be shared with others, particularly with members of his or her household. Such sharing would help everyone to be on the same page while discussing issues relating to the creation of a functional domestic church.

The purpose of publishing three volumes of this book on the same subject and releasing all three at the same time is to make resource materials readily available to parents, grandparents, catechists, teachers, seminarians, elders, youths, etc., who want to develop their domestic church and family spirituality as well as use the volumes to teach different categories of people in the Church, in the homes, seminaries or as reference materials for conferences, workshops and seminars.

While Volume One lays bare the preparatory ground for the development of faith in the domestic church, Volumes Two and Three have been written to help the reader to reflect deeply on issues on a higher ground of our mission on earth and what is to be done by us individually and collectively in order to be where our Lord Jesus Christ wants us to be when our stay in this world has ended. It is to bring this message to every doorstep that I reflected on the following topics in Volume One:

(a) how the Holy Family Society, which is currently engaged in the new evangelisation mission of the Church came into existence and its faith-building projects

(b) why the Holy Family Society's mission is to return families to God

(c) why the family as a domestic church requires daily development

(d) the need to prepare family members for the journey of faith

(e) sustaining the domestic church and the roles of family members

(f) promoting Christian values in a domestic church.

(g) what to learn in the domestic church for family evangelisation

(h) making useful friends to help develop one's domestic church.

(i) review of Volume One and previews of Volumes Two and Three, followed by three appendices: Order of Mass, some selected songs of the Holy Family Society and historic pictures taken at the World Meeting of Families.

Contents of Volumes Two and Three

Now the reader has had a refresher on the contents of Volume One, there is also the need to look on to the higher gains that can come from the mission that God has given to each and every one of us. In this Volume Two, which the reader has probably finished reading to this point, what should immediately come to mind is that this volume has essentially dealt with the need to have a functioning domestic church for the spiritual benefit of everyone in the household. It has also placed emphasis on the importance of attending the World Meeting of Families, with a view to developing our domestic church.

Volume Three, which is an offshoot of this, is indisputably a 'must read'. The reader will find that mainly focuses on the universal call to holiness and what it takes to achieve this in the family. All the topics are treated in such a way that family members will learn much about sainthood and how some married couples have become saints. This is meant to encourage married couples in the world to take their marital vocation seriously by making effective use of their domestic church and doing ordinary things in the society in an extraordinary manner by giving attention to detail.

Members of the family are therefore expected to look at the higher gains that come from the individual response to the universal call to holiness and the steadfast struggle that will bring those who do God's will here on earth to the 'narrow gate' through which they can joyfully pass to heaven. Families should also know that it is quite a higher gain and a thing of great joy to have priests and/or reverend sisters coming out of well-ordered Christian and non-Christian homes.

To make this message clear and encourage people to endeavour to have well-ordered Christian homes, the reader is further introduced to certain fundamentals that can help families to make their domestic church not only functional but also successful in preparing members of their own families for effective Christian mission in God's vineyard.

I do not find it not out place to make the reader aware that as we strive every day to attend to our family issues, as well as participate in

Church activities and societal duties, we must at the same time take valuable steps to prepare ourselves for a holy death. I would indicate that it is only when we effectively prepare for this that we will find ourselves ready to be welcomed by the Holy Family in heaven when our own time is up here on earth. To justify the position of the scriptures and the Church in these matters, as well as the reason for the Holy Family Society to adopt the same, it is necessary to bring in Volume Three of the book in order to make reflections on the various topics quite expansive and beneficial to both Christian and non-Christian families.

The new topics therefore dealt with in Volumes Two and Three, which the reader may want to read and recommend to others, include the following:

Volume Two:
The Family as a Domestic Church: Experiences From the World Meeting of Families

Volume Three:
The Domestic Church: The Way to Holiness and to a Holy Death

Taking up Your Cross and Following Jesus

Having given a bird's eye view of what the reader is to expect in Volume Three, I would invite all Christians and non-Christians alike to use every available opportunity to pay frequent visits to the Blessed Sacrament where they can truly experience peace of mind and body. By doing this, our Lord Jesus Christ will draw the regular visitor to himself.

How can this happen, the reader may want to ask here? This can be briefly explained by letting the reader know that Jesus' love for humanity is overwhelming. He wants us to live perpetually in peace, hence the first few words he uttered and shared with the Apostles and by extension, with all of us, after his resurrection were: 'Peace be with you' (Jn 20:19).

It is this same peace that he extends to us every day as we visit him in the Blessed Sacrament. His manifest presence there is not in doubt since it is the consecrated host that Christ describes as his own body that is placed there in the tabernacle.

Before the priest places the consecrated host in the tabernacle, he goes through the spiritual ceremony that Christ instituted at the Last Supper. To assure his Apostles and indeed all of us that he was not going to leave us as orphans, Christ instituted the Holy Eucharist in the presence of his Apostles as 'he took bread, and when he had given thanks, broke it and gave it to them, saying, "This my body which is given for you. Do this in remembrance of me". And likewise the chalice after supper, saying, "This chalice which is poured out for you is the new covenant in my blood'" (Lk 22:19–20).

The anointed priest of God has the power flowing from Christ himself to perform this ceremony to make Christ really present in the consecrated host placed in the tabernacle. This is why Christ is there waiting for us to visit him every day to leave our worries and anxieties at his feet. He invites us to come to him when he says, 'Come to me, all who labour and are heavy laden, and I will give you rest. Take my yoke upon you, and learn from me; for I am gentle and lowly in heart, and you will find rest for your souls. For my yoke is easy and my burden light' (Mt 11:28–30).

To further assure us that he is there to attend to our needs, he says, 'Ask it will be given to you; seek and you will find; knock, it will be opened to you. For every one who asks receives, and he who seeks, finds, and for him who knocks, it will be opened' (Mt 7:7–8).

If we believe this and take our problems to our Lord Jesus Christ, the scripture also assures us that: 'No one who believes in him will be put to shame' (Rm 10:11). It is therefore the author's recommendation that those who believe in Jesus Christ should make it a habit to always find time to visit the Blessed Sacrament, more so as Christ further reveals to us; 'I am the light of the world; he who follows me will not walk in darkness, but will have the light of life' (Jn 8:12). So, if we allow Jesus to take complete control of our lives and follow his footsteps as we walk along with him, we will be in perpetual light and therefore, we will not experience darkness in our lives.

The other reason we need to follow Jesus, walk along with him and be in his presence all the time, whether we are at home, in the Church, in the school, in the marketplace or on the road is that Jesus says to us at every point in time: 'I am the Way and the Truth and the Life; no one comes to the father, but by me' (Jn 14:6). Having known this, it becomes very instructive that we should lean on him who will eventually take us to his Father in heaven.

So, for us to contemplate Jesus all the time and be in his presence, we need to help ourselves by having certain spiritual tools that can help us contemplate him individually and collectively, and also feel his presence. To enable us to do this from time to time, especially when we are in the presence of the Blessed Sacrament, I have reproduced the prayers that family members can use when they are before the Blessed Sacrament. These same prayers could also be used in the domestic church where there is no opportunity to have exposition of the Blessed Sacrament.

What we need to realise is that Christ himself has assured us that 'where two or three are gathered in my name, there am I in their midst' (Mt 18:20). This makes it important for family members to always come together to pray in their private chapel or in a place designated for prayers in their homes. Apart from the usual family prayers that family members say at home, they could also have some days set apart for everyone to have Family Holy Hour Devotion. It is to help promote this devotion that we have included, in this volume, the prayers specially compiled by Fr Ed Debany, SJ, for family use. This is reproduced below as Appendix A.

It is appropriate to remind the reader here that the Holy Mass is the apex of all prayers. Therefore, to ensure active participation at Mass, I have deemed it necessary to have the Order of Mass reproduced in both Volumes One and Three of this book. The three volumes of this book have, understandably, been prepared as 'companion books' to accompany the reader to his or her prayer meeting in the home, and to the Church anywhere in the world, especially when the reader is going to participate in the celebration of the Holy Eucharist, and the Holy Hour Adoration.

Feast of Pope St John Paul II
22 October 2020, Miami, Florida
Sir David E. Osunde
Founder/National Coordinator, Holy Family Society

Appendices

Appendix A
PRIVATE ADORATION

FAMILY HOLY HOUR WITH BENEDICTION OF THE BLESSED SACRAMENT

EXPOSITION *(In the Church or when a priest is present in a family home to do the exposition.*
Please kneel as the priest exposes the Blessed Sacrament)

Opening Hymn: We Adore You ...
Godhead here in hiding, whom we do adore,
masked by these bare shadows, shape and nothing more;
See lord at Thy service, low lies here a heart,
Lost are we in wonder, at the God Thou art.

Seeing, touching, tasting, are in thee deceived
How says trusty hearing, that shall be believed.
What God's Son has told me, take for truth I do,
Truth Himself speaks truly, or there's nothing true!

Jesus whom I look at, shrouded here below,
I beseech Thee send me what I thirst for so.
Someday to look upon Thee, face to face in light;
And be blest forever, with Thy glory's sight.

Adore Devote – Latin
Adore Devote, lantes Deitas,
Quae sub his figures vere latitas:
Tibi se cor meum totum subjicit
Qui ad te comtemplans, totum deficit.

Visus, tactus, gustus, in te fallitur
Sed auditu solo, tuto creditur.
Credo quidquid dixit Dei filius:
Nil hoc verbo veri-tatis, verius.

Jesus quem velatum, nunc aspicio,
Oro fiat illud, quid tam sitio:
Ut te revelata cernens facie,
Visus sim beatus, tuae gloriae. Amen.

OPENING PRAYER BEFORE THE BLESSED SACRAMENT

(ALL) Oh Lord Jesus Christ, it is your great Love for mankind that keeps you day and night in this Sacrament, full of pity and love, expecting, inviting and welcoming all who visit you. We believe that you are really present in the Sacrament of the altar. We adore you and thank you for the graces you have given to us as members of the Holy Family Society, especially for the gift of yourself in this Sacrament. We intercede with you for our family members here present – both young and old, healthy and sick – as well as those not physically present with us at this time.

May no worries or distractions keep us from looking upon you most Blessed of all Sacraments. Accept our weariness and tiredness. You who promised to refresh and strengthen all who are burdened and wearied by life's challenges and temptations, refresh us and our family members with your Passion. Help us not to be weary nor to fall asleep as did the Apostles, Peter, James and John, in the Garden of Gethsemane. Help us Lord Jesus, to be alert as we pray for the sanctification of our Church, our nation, Nigeria, and other nations of the world, and especially for the unity and sanctification of our families.

Oh Jesus, Bread of Life, food of angels and of men, may our adoration of you make us a better, more generous and kinder people. May it form us and mould us to act as you once behaved with your Mother Mary and St Joseph, in the Holy Family of Nazareth. Amen.

LITANY OF THE HOLY FAMILY

The Leader chants or recites the Litany. The people respond with: **Have mercy on us**

Leader: Lord have mercy **(Repeat)** + Christ have mercy **(Repeat)** + Lord have mercy **(Repeat)**

Leader: Jesus hear us, **People:** Jesus graciously hear us.

God the Father of Heaven,
(All respond: Have mercy on us),

+ God the Son, Redeemer of the World,

+ God the Holy Spirit,

+ Holy Trinity, One God,

+ Holy Family, model of family life, (**All respond: Pray for us**)

+ Holy Family, most meek, humble and devout,

+ Holy Family, most wise, patient and obedient,

+ Holy Family, most pure, chaste and caring,

+ Holy Family, most faithful, courageous and powerful,

+ Holy Family, most prudent, generous and vulnerable,

+ Abyss of peace, love and unity,

+ Possessor and dispenser of all graces,

+ Freedom of captives and comforter of the afflicted,

+ Help of Christians and Health of the sick,

+ Conversion of sinners and Returner of the exiles,

+ Freedom of the Souls in Purgatory,

+ Victor over demons and powers,

+ Protector and provider of the poor,

+ Comfort of widows and orphans,

+ Power of fertility and safe delivery,

+ Protector and good shepherd of families,

+ Chain binding all couples,

+ End of all battles.

Lamb of God, who takes away the sins of the world, **(Spare us O Lord)**

Lamb of God, who takes away the sins of the world, **(Graciously hear us O lord**)

Lamb of God, who takes away the sins of the world, **(Have mercy on us)**

Leader: Jesus Christ hear us,
People: Jesus Christ graciously hear us.

Leader: Pray for us O Holy Family.
People: That we may be made worthy of the promises of our God.

(ALL) Almighty Father, you have made the Holy Family of Jesus, Mary and Joseph to be the model of all family life, grant all our families the grace to imitate them so as to please, praise and glorify you and at the end be welcomed into your Kingdom where you live and reign with Jesus and the Holy Spirit, one God for ever and ever. Amen.

PRAYER AGAINST EVIL SPIRITS, FORCES AND TEMPTATIONS!
(ALL) O Sacrament Most Holy, O Sacrament Divine, all praise and all thanksgiving, be every moment thine! Amen. (brief pause).

O God – Father, Son and Holy Spirit, Most Holy Trinity, Immaculate Virgin Mary, Angels, Archangels and Saints of Heaven, descend upon us as we kneel before the Blessed Sacrament of love and healing. Please purify us Lord, mould us, fill us with yourself, use us. Banish all the forces of evil from our families, destroy them, vanquish them so that we may be healthy and do the good deeds we want to do while refusing to do the bad deeds we so detest. Banish from our family members both present and absent all spells, witchcraft, evil spirits, demons, diabolic infestations, oppressions and possessions; all that is evil and sinful – lack of trust, selfishness, disobedience, envy, pride, psychological, moral, spiritual and diabolic ailments. Drive all these evils away from us and our household, that they may not disturb us nor our loved ones. Jesus, whom we look at present upon this altar, we ask that you command all the forces that vex us as family, *to leave us* and to be consigned into everlasting hell where they will be bound by Saint Michael, the Archangel, and crushed under the heel of the Immaculate Virgin Mary, Mother of the Holy Family and Queen of Nigeria. **(Here pause for one minute silent adoration)**.

INTERCESSORY PRAYER TO MARY, MOTHER OF THE HOLY EUCHARIST
NOTE: *Here follows the slow, meditative recitation of one decade of the Holy Rosary keeping in mind ten different people or situations that we want to bring to Jesus for his attention. Pray especially for family members most in need of our Lady's intercession.*

Pause briefly between each Hail Mary while also thinking of the person or situation to pray for. This may be followed by Morning or Evening Prayer from the Divine Office Book.

BENEDICTION HYMNS
Down in adoration falling
This Great Sacrament we hail.
Over ancient forms of worship,
Newer rites of Grace prevail,
Faith will tell us Christ is present,
When our human senses fail.

To the Everlasting Father
And the Son who made us free,

And the Spirit, God proceeding
From them each eternally.
Be Salvation, Honour, Blessing
Height and endless Majesty.
Amen.

LATIN

Tantum ergo Sacramentum
Veneremur cernui
Et anticum documentum
Novo cedat ritui
Praestet fides supplementum
Sensuum defectui.

Genitori genitoque
Laus et iubilatio
Salus, Honour, Virtus Quoque
Sit et Benedictio
Procedenti ab utroque
Compar sit laudatio.
Amen.

Priest: Panem de caelo praestitisti eis.
(You have given us Bread from Heaven)
People: Omne delectamentum in se habentem.
(Having all sweetness within it)

Priest: Oremus: Deus, qui nobis sub Sacramentum mirabili
Passionis tuae memoriam reliquisti; tribue quaesumus ita nos
Corporis et Sanguinis tui sacra mysteria venerari, ut
redemptionis tuae fructum in nobis iugiter sentiamus. Qui vivis
et regnas in saecula saeculorum. Amen.

(In English) *Let us pray: Oh Lord our God, you have left us in this wonderful Sacrament, a memorial of your Passion and Resurrection, help us we beg you, to reverence the Mystery of your Body and Blood, that we may always experience the fruits of your Salvation. You who live and reign for ever and ever. Amen.*

THE DIVINE PRAISES

Blessed be God.
Blessed be His Holy Name.
Blessed be Jesus Christ, true God and true Man.
Blessed be the Name of JESUS.
Blessed be His most Sacred Heart.
Blessed be His most Precious Blood.
Blessed be Jesus Christ, in the most Holy Sacrament of the Altar.
Blessed be the Holy Spirit the Paraclete.
Blessed be the Great Mother of God, Mary most Holy.
Blessed be Her holy and Immaculate Conception.
Blessed be Her Glorious Assumption.
Blessed be the Name of Mary, Virgin and Mother.
Blessed be St Joseph, Her most Chaste Spouse.
Blessed be God in His Angels and in His Saints.

ADOREMUS et LAUDATE (We adore and praise You O Blessed Sacrament)

Priest (only): Adoremus in Aeternum, Sanctissimum Sacramentum.
People: Repeat ...
Priest (only): Laudate Dominum omnes gentes Laudate eum omnes populi.
People: Quoniam confirmata est super nos misericordia eius; et veritas Domini manet in aeternum.
Priest: Gloria Patri et Filio, et Spiritui Sancto
+ Sicut erat in principio, et nunc et semper. et in saecula saeculorum. Amen.

People: Adoremus in Aeternum, Sacramentum, Sanctissimum Sacramentum.

SALVE REGINA (Hail Holy Queen)
Salve Regina, Mater misericordia, Vita dulcedo et spes nostra salve. Ad te clamamus, exules Filii Evae ad te suspiramus, gemente et flentes, in hac lacrimarum valle. Eia ergo, advocata nostra Illos tuos misericordes oculos, ad nos converte, Et Iesum, benedicum fructum ventris tui. Nobis, post hoc exilium ostende, O clemens, O pia, O dulcis Virgo Maria.

Priest: Pray for us O Holy Mother of God.
People: That we may be made worthy of the promises of Christ.

Let us pray: O God, Our refuge and our strength, look down with favour upon your people who cry to you; and by the intercession of the Glorious and Immaculate Virgin Mary, Mother of God, of St Joseph her faithful spouse, of your blessed Apostles, Peter and Paul, and of all the Saints, mercifully and graciously hear the prayers which we pour forth for the conversion of sinners, and for the liberty and exultation of our Holy Mother, the Church, through the same Christ our Lord. Amen.
Our Lady Queen of Nigeria – Pray for us!
Holy Family: Make our family like yours!
Jesus, Mary and Joseph: Protect our family and save the souls of all the faithful departed!
Holy Family: Be our model and our inspiration!

Closing Hymn: Holy Queen We Bend Before Thee
1. Holy Queen we bend before thee
Queen of purity divine
Make us love thee we implore thee
Make us truly to be thine.

R. Teach, oh teach us Holy Mother how to conquer every sin. How to love and help each other, how the price of life to win.

2. Thou to whom a child is given
Greater than the sons of men
Coming down from highest heaven
To create the world again. **R**

NOTE: *Fr Ed Debany, SJ who compiled the prayer for the Family Holy Hour above, was assigned by his Regional Superior to work with the Holy Family Society in 2012, during which time he accompanied this author to attend the Seventh World Meeting of Families that took place in Milan, Italy. He took most of the historic pictures the reader will find in Appendix C below.*

Appendix B
SELECTED HOLY FAMILY SONGS/HYMNS

(May be used after each decade of the Holy Rosary and at Mass)

(1) Here We Are Lord (Communion Song)

CHORUS:
Here we are Lord to answer your call,
Make our Family like yours
And let the Holy Family be our true model.

1. Jesus, the Way, the Truth and Life
   Calls families to imitate
   His Family of Nazareth.
   Are you ready?

2. Jesus, Comforter of the weak
   Invites your own Family
   To meet him for strength and love
   Are you ready?

3. Jesus, present in the Eucharist
   Gives his body and blood
   To nourish our body and soul
   Are you ready?

4. Jesus, the hope of all mankind
   Gives long time to you and me
   To amend our lives each night and day
   Are you ready?

(2) And So Help Me Lord

CHORUS:
And so help me Lord, help me Lord
To model my life after Jesus, Mary and Joseph,

And so help me Lord.
Please, help me Lord, help me Lord
To model my life after Jesus, Mary and Joseph,
And so help me Lord.

1. In my life, I have chosen Jesus, Mary and Joseph
   as a model,
   A model for parents and children,
   Model for you and for me.

2. Holy lifestyle is a model,
   Model for you and for me,
   A model for the young and old,
   Model for everyone in Christ.

3. Their virtues of obedience and simple life,
   demonstrate to all, on this earth,
   That we need the same virtues,
   To lead us to God.

4. Their virtues of love, and self-giving,
   Show us the truth, that in all things,
   That the will of God,
   must forever prevail.

5. Their virtues of patience, and self-commitment,
   Show us the way, that on our journey
   That we need the same qualities,
   To lead us to God.

(3) Holy Family, The Noble Family

CHORUS:
Holy Family ... the noble family,
Give me support, to have the strength,
The courage and the love
To do God's will just like you

1. Jesus the Son of God
   Your love is what I need
   To return to my Father
   In joy and in peace.

2. Mary the Mother of God
   Your courage is what I need
   To return to my Father
   In peace and obedience.

3. Joseph, the carpenter,
   Your strength is what I need
   To return to my Father
   In love and patience.

4. Jesus, the Comforter,
   Your wisdom is what I need
   To return to my Father
   In courage and strength.

5. Mary, the Queen of Heaven
   Your love is what I need
   To return to my Father
   In strength and breadth.

6. Joseph, the breadwinner
   Your faith is what I need
   To return to my Father
   In trust and strength.

(4) Knowing Jesus, Mary and Joseph

CHORUS:
Knowing Jesus, Mary and knowing Joseph,
Is my joy every day, every day
Knowing the Holy Family is the joy of my family,
Knowing the Holy Family of Nazareth,

Is what we must do
To have joy in our heart,
And joy in our home.

1. Every day, I take time to read the scripture
   To know more about the Holy Family
   What about you my dear friend?

2. Every day, my family reflects
   On the virtues of Jesus, Mary and Joseph
   What about you my dear friend?

3. Every day, I struggle to practice
   The virtues of the Holy Family
   What about you my dear friend?

4. Every day, I depend on the Holy Family
   To improve my own spirituality
   What about you my dear friend?

5. Every day, I call on the Holy Family
   To show me the way to the Father
   What about you my dear friend?

6. Every day, I kneel down to bless
   The Holy Family for my own life
   What about you my dear friend?

7. Every day, I call on the Holy Family
   And my hands are blessed with gifts
   What about you my dear friend?

NOTE: The above songs can also be sung at different Christian ceremonies to honour Jesus, Mary and Joseph, the Holy Family of Nazareth.

Appendix C
PHOTOGRAPHIC SECTION
Activities of the Osundes with Pope John Paul II (canonised as Saint), Pope Benedict XVI (Emeritus), Pope Francis, Apostolic Nuncios in Nigeria and some Nigerian Catholic Bishops at different local and international events, all aimed at building and promoting the Catholic faith

Family/Personal Pictures of the Contributors of the True-Life Stories to This Work

Above left: Clemetina Osunde who experienced a lot when she accompanied her dad and other family members to the World Meeting of Families in Dublin, Ireland, in 2018. See her story pp. 88–90.

Above right: The family picture of Miss Glenda Oloke (second left). She also went to the World Meeting of Families in Dublin, Ireland in 2018, with her mum, Mrs Augusta Oloke (far left). Her father, Engr Godwin Oloke, is standing far right. Glenda relates her inspirational story pp. 91–93.

Dr Mrs Marian Imaze Davis (far left), together with her husband, Tyree (beside her), and their children who accompanied them to the World Meeting of Families in Milan, Italy, in 2012. Dr Marian Imaze Davis narrates her family experiences pp. 101–109.

The faithfully growing family of Mrs Ivonne Ruiz, resident in Miami, Florida, who relies heavily on prayer and the practice of togetherness in the family. She tells her family story pp. 98–99.

The story of Mrs Georgiana Ogbutor, and her blossoming family, is joyfully narrated on pp. 99–101. Here, she sits comfortably with her husband, with both of them carrying their grandchildren. What a happily married life to behold!

Local/International Activities of the Holy Family Society

In the following photos: some fruitful results of the activities of the Holy Family Society, culminating in the ordination of some of her members in the major seminaries as priests, the growth of faith of family members and the conversion of many others to the Catholic faith.

Rev Fr C. Ugorji, Natinional Chaplain of the Holy Family Society (standing far right) joins hands with some members of the society to present a special gift to a newly ordained priest, Rev Fr Bruno Frank Ogoke, MSP, (third from right) after a well-attended Mass of Ordination in Gwagwalada, Abuja. Rev Fr B. F. Ogoke, MSP, was an active member of the Holy Family Society during his seminary days.

Rev Fr C. C. Ugorgi , Esq, National Chaplain of the Holy Family Society, (centre) with some members of the society, after concelebrating at the Ordination Mass in which four members of the society were ordained as priests at the National Seminary of the Missionary Society of St Paul, Gwagwadala, Abuja, Nigeria.

Here, Sir David E. Osunde, leader of the Holy Family Society delegation to the Cameroon, briefs participating members which include Rev Fathers, Rev Sisters and lay persons on details of their evangelisation mission to the Cameroon in 2013.

Pope Benedict XVI who appointed Sir David and Dame Mary-Joan Osunde as members of the Pontifical Council for the Family in 2009, is seen here receiving the Osundes in one of the Vatican events during his papacy.

Happy historic moments recorded by Rev Fr Ed Debany SJ, the Spiritual Project Director of the Holy Family Society in 2012, who did a special coverage report on the participation of the Holy Family Society at the five-day world event in Milan, Italy, on his return to Nigeria.

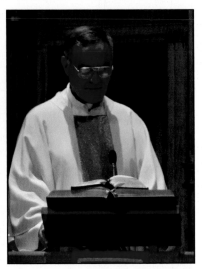

Mr Tyree Davis and his wife, Dr (Mrs) Marian Imaze Davis came in from Florida, USA, to attend the World Meeting of Families in Milan in 2012. A report on the family's spirit-filled visit is reported on pp 101 to 109.

Rev Fr Ed Debany, SJ, who went with the Holy Family Society delegation to Milan, Italy, in 2012, used the occasion to pray fervently for the projects of the Holy Family Society.

Bibliography

Bishop Emmanuel Adetoyese Badejo, 'The Influence of Modern Media and New Ideologies on the Family in Africa Today', Symposium of Episcopal Conferences for Africa and Madagascar, Angola, 2012

Compendium of the Social Doctrine of the Church to His Holiness Pope John Paul II Master of Social Doctrine and Evangelical Witness to Justice and Peace, Vatican, 2004

Craig, D., *Philly Voice*, 'Transcript of Pope Francis' Improvised Festival of Families Speech', 27 September 2015, https://www.phillyvoice.com/transcript-pope-francis-festival-families-speech/; accessed on 2 July 2020

Eitzen, D.S., Baca-Zin, M., *Social Problems*, 8th edn, Boston: Allyn and Bacon, 2002

Fagan, P., *The Heritage Foundation*, 'Why Religion Matters Even More: The Impact of Religious Practice on Social Stability', https://www.heritage.org/civil-society/report/why-religion-matters-even-more-the-impact-religious-practice-social-stability; accessed on 22 November 2021

Macionis, J., *Sociology*, 13th edn, New Jersey: Pearson Education Inc., 2010

Pope Francis, *Address to Participants in the 37th National Convocation of the Renewal in the Holy Spirit*, Rome, 2014

Pope Francis, *Angelus* on 20 September 2020, Vatican, 2020

Pope Francis, Apostolic Exhortation *Evangelii Gaudium*, Vatican, 2013

Pope Francis, Apostolic Exhortation *Gaudete et Exsultate*, Vatican, 2018

Pope Francis, Apostolic Letter issued *Motu Propio, As a Loving Mother*, Vatican, 2016

Pope Francis, Apostolic Letter issued *Motu Propio, Vos Estis Lux Mundi*, Vatican, 2019

Pope Francis, General Audience 4 October 2017, Vatican, 2017

Pope Francis, General Audience 13 November 2019, Vatican, 2019

Pope Francis, *Letter of His Holiness Pope Francis to the People of God*, Vatican, 2018

Pope Francis, *Message of His Holiness Pope Francis for the 54th World Communications Day*, Rome, 2020

Pope Francis, Post-Synodal Apostolic Exhortation *Amoris Laetitia*, Vatican, 2016

Pope John Paul II, Apostolic Exhortation *Familiaris Consortio*, Vatican, 1981

Pope John Paul II, Apostolic Letter *Novo Millennio Inuente*, Vatican, 2001

Pope John Paul II, Apostolic Pilgrimage to Bangladesh, Singapore, Fiji Islands, New Zealand, Australia and Seychelles *Homily of Pope John Paul II* on 30 November 1986, Perth, Australia, 1986

Pope John Paul II, Post-Synodal Apostolic Exhortation *Ecclesia in Africa*, Vatican, 1995

Pope Paul VI, *Address in Nazareth*, Nazareth, 1964

Pope Paul VI, Dogmatic Constitution on the Church *Lumen Gentium*, Vatican, 1964

Slater, S., *Stand for the Family*, Family Watch International, 2010

St Augustine of Hippo, *De Trinitate, c.* 1200–99

The Holy Bible, Revised Standard Version, 2nd Catholic edn

Vatican Archive, *Catechism of the Catholic Church*, https://www.vatican.va/archive/ENG0015/_INDEX.HTM; accessed on 9 August 2021

Grandparents and parents, know that it is your innate responsibility to bring your loved ones under the protective canopy of Jesus, Mary and Joseph, the Model Family for the world, and you will remain eternally grateful to God, if you do. As you lovingly take this message to heart and share same to grandparents and parents who cross your path, this author is wishing you and your loved ones as well as all grandparents and parents God's infinite love and overwhelming spiritual care for taking positive steps to bring your own families under the ever growing, protective canopy of the Holy Family of Nazareth.